The
Victorian &
Edwardian
Cotswolds

HOLYWELL FARM LANE, OAKRIDGE

MANOEUVRES AT FULBROOK

The
Victorian &
Edwardian
Cotswolds

Alan Sutton

AMBERLEY

TETBURY

First published 1990 under the title *The Cotswolds of 100 Years Ago*
This revised edition first published 2008

Amberley Publishing
Cirencester Road, Chalford,
Stroud, Gloucestershire, GL6 8PE

British Library Cataloguing in Publication Data.
A catalogue record for this book is available from the British Library.

ISBN 978-1-84868-017-3

Typesetting and origination by Amberley Publishing
Printed in Great Britain by Asterim

Preface

With this book, *The Victorian & Edwardian Cotswolds*, my aim is to bring some of the best photographs together, with contemporary text to illustrate visually and expressively the conditions in which the ordinary folk of the Cotswolds lived their daily lives. I derive great pleasure when poring over the many different faces in old photographs, and see these people, young and old, a few seconds of their life in an image, an encapsulation of a moment long gone: the people who lived in the houses and cottages of the Cotswolds in late Victorian and early Edwardian times.

It must be because of my personal sense of history that I cannot look at a building and see it just as it is today. When driving through the Stroud valleys, passing Cotswold stone cottages that housed weavers and their families, or grander, gabled houses that were built with style and confidence by the clothiers of the area, I cannot but reflect upon my predecessors – the generations before us who built these dwellings – their joys and sorrows, and the mark they have left upon this beautiful part of England.

The pictures and text, which illustrate the influence these Cotswold folk had on their surroundings vary in date from the 1860s to the 1920s, but the majority are from the period between 1880 and 1900. The reader should therefore understand that some licence has been taken with both photographs and extracts in order to give a broader flavour of life in this area at that time. In the same sense, the text is all 'local', but the locality is not precisely limited to the Cotswold hills. As an example, to get the best coverage in content I have strayed slightly to the south-east to include the Revd Francis Kilvert and Alfred Williams, who together give us great expressive insight into the life of ordinary rural people at the end of the last century. The area covered photographically is all within sight of the Cotswolds, but is bounded on the west by the Severn, and on the east by the Thames Valley.

The majority of inhabitants in this Cotswold region were workers; agricultural and industrial. On the wolds jobs were largely on the land, while in the valleys they were mainly in industry. Some woollen mills still existed, but in the buildings vacated by failed clothiers new industries developed to employ the large population which had grown out of the clothing trade. Because of this essential focus on the working classes, there is only token representation and documentation of the other strata of society.

In the nineteenth century the country was run by a small, privileged minority who espoused ideals of self-help and thrift. The classic example is the introduction of the Union Workhouse with its harsh and

EMPLOYEES OF SELWYN'S FLOCK MILL, TOADSMOOR

GLOUCESTER DOCKS

authoritarian rules, which were purposely deterrent to prevent those whom the Victorians considered to be 'scroungers' benefiting from the assistance given. In reality the truly needy, sick and aged were often refused help, in an effort to keep costs down and reduce parish rates. Some of the accounts moved me to anger, an example being the diary entry by the Revd Francis Kilvert describing the hungry boy (p. 58).

Apart from the painful and the poignant, there are pieces which well describe the changing attitudes during the latter forty years of Queen Victoria's reign. These years are particularly well summarized by Major Gambier-Parry, who, although a member of the 'establishment' was nevertheless well able to describe the subtle nuances of change as the old order disappeared and more materialistic attitudes developed among the working people. Alfred Williams describes his own people and provides wonderful character cameos from the eastern Cotswolds and upper Thames Valley. Laurie Lee's description of his mother remains my favourite piece of prose, and J. Arthur Gibbs delights us with his description of a public election meeting, together with other observations on his local village and its characters. Complementing this idiosyncratic collection are the dialect writings of John Drinkwater, S.S. Buckman and Edmund Hall. This selection illustrates the wealth of local language which we have almost entirely lost, so much so that I felt it was necessary to include a glossary for 'translation' at the end of this book. So, do 'e come wi' I to the end of this preface to thank the many yolk as 'ave lent 'and in this yur buk.

The compilation of this book has given me great satisfaction and I hope in turn that it will give pleasure to many thousands of people in reading. It would not have been possible without the help, encouragement and advise of the following, who through their knowledge and collections have made the project possible: David Aldred, Fred Archer, Lucile Bell, Richard Chidlaw, Edwin Cuss, Donald Emes, David E. Evans, Brian Frith, John V. Garrett, Malcolm Graham, Stanley Gardiner, Philip Griffiths, Kate Haslem, Charles Hilton, Alfred Jewell, Laurie Lee, Wilfred Merrett, John Phillips, Jean Price, Rosemary Verey, David Viner, Jill Voyce, Roger Whiting, Tom Worley, and the staffs of Cotswold District Council (Cotswold Countryside Collection, Northleach), Gloucestershire Record Office, Gloucestershire County Library (Gloucestershire Collection) and Oxfordshire Library and Museum Services (Local History Library, Westgate).

Finally, I shall let speak for me the wonderful character who was inspired by a Cotswold girl; for it was in a Cotswold village that Charles Lutwidge Dodgson first met Alice Liddell: 'What is the use of a book', thought Alice, 'without pictures or conversations?'

Alan Sutton

Introduction

All things bright and beautiful,
All creatures great and small,
All things wise and wonderful,
The Lord God made them all.

Each little flower that opens,
Each little bird that sings,
He made their glowing colours,
He made their tiny wings.

The rich man in his castle,
The poor man at his gate,
God made them, high or lowly,
And order'd their estate.

The third verse from this hymn by Cecil Alexander, written in 1848, epitomizes the Victorian attitudes towards wealth and poverty. The pre-ordained nature of an individual's level in society was assumed and accepted by most:

'Mornin', James! Fine mornin', James!'
'Fine marnin's no goo wi' no bren cheese in the cubberd, measter,' James answered.

'Good morning, Etherd!
'Oy! Oy! I'm a-gwoin on yander. Some on 'em got girt sticks in ther faggots, but I got none in mine.'

Some people had meat in their broth, Etherd did not, and he was on his way to the workhouse – a poor man at his gate, pre-ordained to his estate.

The watershed that broke this mould was the First World War, and the text in this book therefore represents the end of the peasant era, a centuries' old struggle of the have-nots against the haves.

As early as the 1380s, the awakening of the peasantry and the throwing off of serfdom after the Black Death of the mid-fourteenth century led to the cry of:

When Adam delved, and Eve span,
Who was then a gentleman?

This revolutionary couplet based upon verses from the hermit and mystic Richard Rolle inspired many individuals through the next three centuries. It also partially led to the popular anarchy of the Diggers and the radical objectives of the Levellers at the end of the Parliamentarian Civil War. The Levellers were ahead of their time, and their wish to see the separation of church from state, constitutional and economic reform, together with freedom of worship, was not in accordance with Cromwell's objectives. He firmly quashed these movements; having no intention of changing the social order, merely the leadership of the existing establishment.

Slowly but surely through the seventeenth and eighteenth centuries the gradual levelling of society took place. Hard-won liberties such as the Toleration Act of 1689, which allowed Nonconformists the freedom of following their own style of religious worship, led more and more to the development of Dissenting groups, encompassing a considerable proportion of the working classes.

The control of the establishment was weakening when the shock resulting from the loss of the American

ON TENTERHOOKS IN THE GOLDEN VALLEY

colonies was followed only six years later by that devastating jolt for monarchies throughout Europe—the French Revolution. After these events things were never quite the same. The nationalist or jingoistic feeling in England prevented a similar uprising, and the eventual collapse of the revolution and the rise of Napoleon put England on to a war footing with an associated war economy. The wars resulted in the development of a strong central administration in England which then put the existing establishment into an almost impregnable situation which has effectively remained ever since.

At the end of the wars a shattered economy and an enormous national debt, taken together with the desire of landowners and industrialists to maintain or increase their income, put an intolerable burden on the peasantry. Farmers also tried to improve their lifestyle, this being the era of pianos in the parlours of the larger farms. Increasingly these farmers were raising their aspirations, taking themselves from their yeoman roots to the lesser gentry.

On the Cotswolds the local economy had held up reasonably well during the Napoleonic Wars. The clothing industry provided high employment in the Stroud, Dursley and Wotton valleys on the western escarpment, and the effect of this comfortable economy gradually spread further into the Cotswolds. After 1815 confidence amongst clothiers resulted in mills being rebuilt or enlarged, and 1824 and the early months of 1825 were a boom period. In 1825 the weavers struck for more money – with considerable justification. The successful grade of cloth selling from the area was a close-woven broadcloth involving more weft, and therefore more weaving, which was done without an increase in pay.

The next two decades were a stop-go period with confidence interspersed with disappointments, the most notable of these being in 1826 when the boom collapsed into full-scale recession. Several local clothiers failed in the mid-l830s; the most spectacular of these being Edward Sheppard of Uley. Sheppard lived in great splendour at a magnificent house, the Ridge, between Dursley and Wotton, which he had built in 1825. In fairness, Sheppard also paid reasonably high wages, and the relative prosperity of the Stroud valleys was noted by William Cobbett in his *Rural Rides*: '. . . the people seem to have been consistently well off. A pig in every cottage sty; that is the infallible mark of a happy people'. Sheppard's bankruptcy resulted in the Ridge being sold to George Bengough, and Bengough's granddaughter has left an account of childhood at the Ridge in the 1880s (p. 45).

MONK'S MILL, ALDERLEY

The failure of Sheppard's mill put at least a thousand people out of work, and the resulting distress of the Uley area was shared by other escarpment areas which suffered similar failures of clothiers. Such was the distress in the western Cotswolds, especially among the weavers, that a government inquiry was commissioned to report into the condition of the hand-loom weavers, and it shows how in just a few years of poor trade the weavers had suffered greatly since the halcyon days witnessed by Cobbett:

The weavers are much distressed; they are wretchedly off in bedding; witness has seen many cases where the man and wife and as many as seven children have slept on straw, laid on the floor with only a torn quilt to cover them; sometimes he has had occasion to search the houses of some weavers on suspicion of stolen yarn or slinge, and has witnessed very distressing cases; children crying for food, and the parents having neither food nor money in the house, or work to obtain any; he has frequently given them money out of his own pocket to provide them with a breakfast.

These men have a great dread of going to the Poor Houses, and live in constant hope that every day will bring them some work; witness has frequently told them they would be better in the house, and their answer has been 'We would sooner starve.' Witness considers this wretched state stints the children in

CHILDREN AT GLOUCESTER DOCKS

LONG STREET, DURSLEY

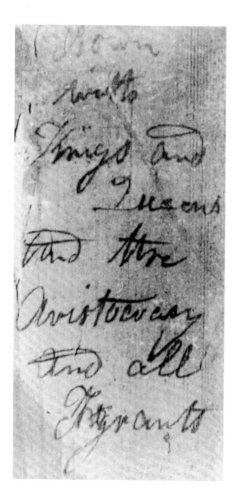

growth, and causes a deal of sickness; does not think that one family out of ten children and adults can attend church, in consequence of their tagged condition; has often dropped in at meal times and found them eating potatoes with a bit of flick or suet.

The fear of the workhouse was not without some justification. The radical Poor Law reforms of 1836 were the result of a determined effort by the comfortably-off Tory establishment to reduce the demand on their pockets occasioned by the parish poor rates. The new Act gathered parishes into 'Unions', and rather than the poor and distressed being given 'outdoor' relief, they were forced to starve, or go to the workhouse, where a regime was put in place purposely to make them as harsh and unappealing as possible.

In 1832, when the reform was under discussion, the Revd H.H. Milman wrote to Edwin Chadwick, Secretary of the Poor Law Commission: 'The workhouse should be a place of hardship, of coarse fare, of degradation and humility; it should be administered with strictness – with severity; it should be as is consistent with humanity . . .'

Needless to say Milman was of the Church of England, and not a Dissenting minister! His view carried the day, and in the Gloucestershire Cotswolds parishes united to form the workhouses of Cirencester,

Cheltenham, Dursley, Gloucester, Stroud and Stow. The rules were cruel, the regime was hard. And although by the 1880s the rules had softened and the whole regime mellowed, the basic principle carried right through to the 1930s (see p. 53).

Charles Dickens was not exaggerating when he drew attention to the plight of the poor in the workhouse in *Oliver Twist*. He was genuinely appalled at the severity of the regime, and many shared his view, but they failed to change opinions, and the better-off elements of society turned a deaf ear. 'Society' could justify its stance by referring to Captain Swing, the mythical leader of the 'Swing' riots of 1830, when hungry, homeless and unemployed people fired ricks, broke machinery and swore dark, unmentionable oaths to obtain a living or destroy the Government:

> Ye gods above, send down your love,
> With swords as sharp as sickles,
> To cut the throats of gentlefolks,
> Who rob the poor of victuals.

The riots were crushed and the Poor Law came into effect. Starvation was no excuse for breaking the law; double standards are easy when you have a full belly.

The Corn Laws of 1815 only allowed importation when the price reached as high as 80 *s.* a quarter. This legislation was purely for the protection of farmers and landowners, and the effect on the working classes does not appear to have been material in the decision-making. The legislation was changed in 1828 and 1842, introducing sliding scales as the result of social unrest, and the Act was repealed in 1846; not through any sense of altruism towards the poor, but more one suspects through fear of revolutions and the effectiveness of the Anti-Corn-Law League. The European revolution of 1848 did not ignite and unify the unrest among the poor in England, although this was much feared by the government. However, unrest there most certainly was, and evidence of it was discovered in Stroud during the 1970s when alterations were being made to Hawkwood College. The college was built as a large country house, the Grove, and in 1845 it was substantially enlarged and 'beautified' by its owner, William Capel. Little did Capel know that one of his artisan carpenters was a revolutionary, a Chartist who scribbled these words on to a cupboard post before fixing it to the wall, a statement of frustration intended like a spellcasting talisman: 'Down with Kings and Queens and the Aristocracy And all Tyrants.'

The industrial depression of 1839–42, together with the Corn Laws, led to the 'Hungry Forties', a time of hunger and deprivation which is referred to several times by the narrators in this book. The suffering was in industrial areas alone; throughout the Cotswolds hardship existed, although the weavers and other cloth-workers probably suffered the greatest as they had no recourse to food, unlike some agricultural labourers. William Augustus Miles gives more information in his *Report on the Condition of the Handloom Weavers*:

> Mr Harvey of Horsley says the agricultural labourer was badly off about six months ago; he now gets 8 s. to 9 s. a week in summer, some men as high as 10 s. with their beer. In harvest time 9 s. a week and 3 s. beer is given. The weavers are very distressed. Many applicants say it is impossible to support themselves by weaving. Considers that nothing would relieve this neighbourhood so much as emigration. Population has increased, while trade has been failing. Many shopkeepers have lost their property, and are little better than paupers. Former cottage property, of which the weavers rented greater part, was very valuable. If a weaver can barely support his family, he has not enough to pay rent. Cottage property is not worth holding.

Slowly the situation got better: new industries developed and many thousands of people emigrated to America, Canada and Australia. In Wotton-under-Edge the population in the 1831 census was 5,431, but by 1901 this had reduced by just over a half, at 2,979. Similar sharp drops were recorded throughout the clothing industry area and relieved the pressure on the demand of available employment.

UNION STREET, DURSLEY, MATRON LEADING THE INMATES TO CHURCH

It was not just in the industrialized western escarpment that emigration took place. Young agricultural labourers throughout the Cotswolds took the opportunity of flight to the colonies before the risk of marriage commitment and poverty (p. 115). In addition, a regular policy was adopted of sending orphans and pauper children from the workhouses to emigration committees. How heart-breaking this must have been for families who could not afford to feed their children, to see them sent to a land far away, knowing that in all probability they would never meet again.

The woollen industry recovered in the 1850s, though introduction of new machinery meant that far fewer people were employed. Mills continued to fail, but this was largely through lack of investment. In Wotton and Kingswood alone Monk's Mill failed in 1867, New Mills in 1870, Park Mill in 1880, and Nind Mill in 1897.

Agriculture went through its own form of revolution. New machinery was also introduced here and wages slowly rose, from an average of 9 s. 7 d. in the 1850s to 13 s. 9 d. in 1880. In addition, landowners invested heavily in drainage and many other improvements, but the farmers and labourers were not to be the successful sector of society in late Victorian England. The success was in the big towns, where real spending power increased by a dramatic 60 per cent in the thirty years from 1860 to 1890. The Cotswolds, especially in the north and east, saw no real benefits, and hardship here was continual and severe because the main occupation was on the land. Many have argued that the agricultural depression of the 1870s onwards was due to the delayed impact of the repeal of the Corn Laws.

This lengthy preamble gives an impression of a downtrodden, starving social group with insufficient power or leadership to rise up and strike at the oppressors. This situation was not really so. Deprivation and hardship there certainly was; selfishness among other elements of society there most certainly was: but an alternative solution would never have been easy. Some levelling of wealth would have helped, but only to a small degree. The truth is that there was a fear among the wealthy that their lifestyle was threatened by radicals, resulting in a determined effort to maintain the status quo. Yet, among most of the poor there was a quiet acceptance of their station in life with only a few activists fomenting revolt. There could never have been a happy compromise.

THE 'GRANDE DAME'

The poor in an apparently happy rural community were constantly living under the spectre of the workhouse. The squire would try to be benevolent, but only to a degree. Past a certain point, when lack of physical strength or lack of supporting relatives could provide a living, the only solution was the workhouse. And to prevent too many applying for this option, the workhouse was made a place of hardship where, for instance, elderly couples were purposely separated to live the remainder of their lives apart! It was not deemed possible in the late nineteenth century to extend largesse. Of course, it was possible, but it could not be done within the existing social framework. To do so would have set a precedent which might have opened the floodgates. This explains Francis Kilvert's observation of the starving boy, and the obvious pity he takes on the boy while not offering him sustenance (p. 49).

The collection in this book shows a range of social conditions and views. The wide variety of pieces illustrate rural life on the Cotswolds as it was viewed by contemporary onlookers, and demonstrate that it was not all a tale of woe. Life goes on, and although in the mid-nineteenth century living conditions were probably worse than they had been in the previous two centuries, this was completely inapparent to the workers. They were not educated, had a poor sense of history, and they had very little choice other than taking life as it came. Many went to industrial areas, many emigrated, but this was generally in times of utter distress, which mercifully were not that many, despite the picture that may have been painted. Unlike Ireland, where many starved to death, the poor on the Cotswolds rarely suffered to that extreme.

By the 1890s, the time around which this book concentrates, life was getting better. The farmers were still having a bad time, but this did not cause the distress among the poor that it would have done fifty years previously. Education was theoretically universal after the Education Act of 1870, and, by the 1890s, this resulted in the first literate generation. The year 1884 saw a Franchise Act which allowed many more men (but not women) the right to vote. The slow march of democracy was further advanced by the introduction of the county councils in 1888, which meant a further deterioration in the political power of the landed interest.

One subject which has not been touched upon, and is not generally, is that of domestic servants. The last thirty years of the nineteenth century was the heyday of the servant, providing employment for thousands of girls from poor families. Every middle-class family had at least one servant, and the number employed was regarded as a rough guide to status; there are accounts of hostesses deciding precedence at their dinner table according to the number of servants kept by their guests.

Several diary entries of John Dearman Birchall expound on the servant problem, and it is clear that trouble with servants taxed him with regularity. Birchall was a newcomer to Gloucestershire and lived at Upton St Leonards, near Gloucester. He easily entered county society, and it is apparent that he was troubled when his gardeners could not deliver the variety and regularity of unusual vegetables that he saw dished up at dinner in his regular visits to other households. In 1876 his cook, Mrs Newsholm – the best cook he ever had – gave notice. After investigation Birchall discovered the problem lay with one Sandy, and after giving Sandy notice the whole servant problem became exposed:

October 16

Considered the servant problem. Mrs Newsholm had said that Sandy having left she would not mind coming back. Margaret said Mrs Newsholm was conscientious and well disposed but prejudiced and inclined to listen to tales. Mrs N. said that Sandy's language was shameful and unfit for young girls to hear and he neither could, nor did work, leaving all to the footmen to do. Ann said for long servants had set one another against the place. Even Keen (the head gardener) was unsettled the first year he was here, and told her he had heard tales enough to induce him to leave ten times. Tothill, although a good worker, had never been a friend of the family and never lost an opportunity of saying and hinting and insinuating things against us, and there was no love lost between Tothill and me . . .

The above example is from a large household. On the Cotswolds many of the servants were farm servants and many of the narrators give evidence to these workers and their lifestyles. They included shepherds, carters, dairy maids, foggers and milkers. On the larger farms, apart from household servants, there would have been a kitchen boy, carter's boys, and many other youngsters undergoing a form of apprenticeship (as mentioned in 'Thomas and Jane' p. 42). These boys were hired as servants and in later years would become day labourers, get married, and live in one of the local cottages attached to the farm.

Whether young or old, annually hired farmworkers often made it a practice to change masters frequently; this is highlighted by J. Arthur Gibbs and Alfred Williams (p. 84 & p. 118), and the hiring fairs were high points in the Cotswold calendar. Carters and wagoners were distinguished by having a piece of whipcord twisted round their hats; thatchers wore a fragment of woven straw; shepherds held their sheep-crocks in hand; and domestic servants carried a mop, giving the name to the gathering.

Many country girls entered domestic service in the 'big' house, and a good account of this is given on p. 84, where Laurie Lee describes his mother and her early life. My own grandmother, an exact contemporary with Laurie Lee's mother, did not enter service, but being the eldest in the family had the unenviable task of bringing up her younger brother and sisters after the premature death of her mother.

Much of my interest in the nineteenth century stems from my enchanting visits to this grandmother, Louisa, and my grandfather, Joseph. My other grandparents were modern. They were nearly twenty years younger and lived in a twentieth-century world with all of the related facilities and accoutrements of modern living. But Joseph and Louisa were different. They lived in a brick weaver's house dating back to the eighteenth century. Hill View was detached, sitting in a large garden extending to one acre or more. At the back were the sinister grounds of the Union Workhouse, to the front was Union Street and at the left, The Slad, both streets containing terraced cottages built of Cotswold stone; and behind these, the church tower of Dursley loomed up, close enough for the time to be easily read from the clock-face.

Hill View had large upstairs rooms that would have once held looms. The kitchen was a lean-to structure built shortly after the house itself, with rudimentary stoneware sink and cold-water brass tap, and a token to modernity–a gas stove. The facilities were up the path and round the corner with torn-up newspaper pinned on a nail. The bath was galvanized and hung up outside. The washing-machine was grandmother's hands, the

JOSEPH AND LOUISA, CHRISTMAS DAY 1903

spin-dryer was the mangle, and the whitener was 'blue', the constituent of which I do not profess to know, but which, like indigo, had the power to whiten linen. The sitting-room, leading on from the kitchen and down two steps, was wainscoted and invariably contained a large aspidistra or fern in a brass pot on a table in the window. The fireplace was surrounded by brassware, grandfather's pipe rack, and a pot of spills for pipe-lighting from the coal fire. Grandfather's chair was a large farmhouse chair on the right-hand side of the fire. Grand mother's was on the left: a softer, more comfortable seat. Above her was a large, wall-mounted, colonial wooden-cased clock. But the most fascinating object in the room was a large sepia photograph hung on the wall: a photo graph taken on their wedding day, Christmas Day 1903.

Childhood memories from the early 1950s are bathed in the haze of time; but much of the haze is from my age at the time rather than the number of years that have passed. Grandmother's sitting-room was a salon and Louisa herself was the *grande dame* of the family, her family, extensive and local, with her house, Hill View, the focal point. In this she had taken over the mantle of her grandmother, Betsy Cross, who from the 1860s onwards had ruled supreme as the *grande dame* of that area of town. Grandmother's salon was often filled with old ladies, relations and friends – Victorians all. Great-aunt Gert and Great-aunt Olive I can recall, but the haze of time has blurred the memories of others, although I still see them in my mind.

I remember Great-aunt Gert – ''ere's our Alan, 'ow are you my love, come and give me a kiss' – and then the escape to the garden to wander through the redcurrant and blackcurrant bushes and fruit trees up to the ruins of the workhouse adjoining the garden, and clamber through the overgrown flower beds and broken walls.

The ruins have gone. Hill View has gone. The cottages in The Slad have gone. And my link with the Victorians has gradually faded away; the last, Uncle Art, Louisa's young brother, died in 1986, aged 102.

One hundred years is just four generations and only a little over the average lifespan. How different life has become since the spectre of the workhouse. Two world wars and a social revolution has greatly changed the Cotswolds since the time of our narrators, and the time of my grandparents' childhood.

The Victorian & Edwardian Cotswolds

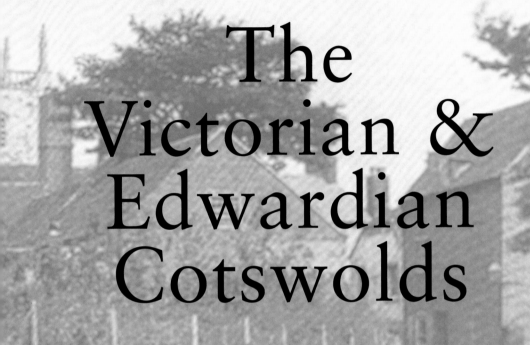

KELL & CO., GLOUCESTER,

SOLE AGENTS FOR THE MASSEY-HARRIS WIDE-OPEN BINDER.

IMPROVED PATENT

HORSE **R**AKES,

☞ HAYMAKERS,

KICKERS,

ELEVATORS,

☞ REAPERS. ☜

AGENTS FOR ALL THE

LEADING

MAKERS

OF

☞ BINDERS.

SPECIALITY:—

PURE MANILLA

BINDER TWINE.

Sample and Price on application.

THE MASSEY-HARRIS WIDE-OPEN BINDER has the GREATEST CAPACITY, and will perform the widest range of work of any SELF-BINDER ever produced. It will work with equal facility in the very SHORTEST or the LONGEST CROPS. It is very LIGHT RUNNING, and is easier on the team than any other Machine. So SIMPLE is the Machine to operate, and so easy to understand, that a BOY capable of handling a team of horses can manage it. The Patent WIDE-OPEN ELEVATOR, with AUTOMATIC FLOATING CANVASS, will elevate crops of any length without shelling the grain. SEND FOR CATALOGUE AT ONCE to

KELL & CO., GLOUCESTER.

JOHN RICHARDS & COMPANY

(LATE JOHN MORSE & SON)

Nurserymen, Seedsmen, & Florists,

◉ DURSLEY. ◉

CUT FLOWERS A SPECIALITY.

We daily supply Wreaths, Crosses, Wedding, Opera, and other Bouquets of the Choicest Hothouse Flowers.

Ladies in the country districts can be supplied with Boxes of Cut Flowers and Fern at 1/6, 2/6, 3/6, 5/-, 7/6, or 10/6, by Post, Rail, or Messenger.

ORNAMENTAL AND OTHER SHRUBS.
◉ FRUIT TREES. ◉
All kinds for the Garden.　　　Standards for Orchards.

Standard and Dwarf Roses.　Bedding Plants in great variety
Palms, Ferns, Orchids.
WHITETHORN FOR QUICK HEDGES.
Grand Assortment of Window Plants always in flower.

DAVID BIRD,

Carpenter, Wheelwright, and Smith,

◉ DURSLEY. ◉

WAGGONS, CARTS, & SPRING CARTS
Made, Repaired, and Painted to Order.

H. LeMAITRE,

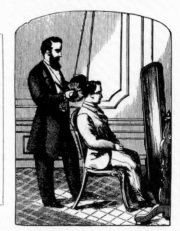

From
R. ALLISTON, Strand, LONDON.

From
SAINT PIERRE, Rue d'Amsterdam, PARIS.

Hair Dresser & Perfumer,

Ladies' and Gentlemen's

HAIR CUTTING, SINGEING, & SHAMPOOING SALLONS,

3, CASTLE STREET, CIRENCESTER.

Ornamental Hair of every description.

Toilet Requisites in great variety.

H. LeMAITRE begs most respectfully to announce that he has Private Rooms and every accommodation for Ladies and Children.

HARPER STREET, TETBURY

BRANDY AT THE RAILWAY

Mr Baker, the Coroner for the Chippenham Division of Wiltshire, held an inquest on Monday, February 16th, on the body of a man named Cornelius Robins, a labourer of this village, who came by his death through cold and exposure, it is presumed brought about by drinking neat brandy in mistake for cider. From the evidence, it appeared that the deceased and a fellow labourer on the same farm, a cripple who was familiarly known as 'Bandy,' were at Malmesbury on Saturday, went into the Railway Hotel, and ordered a pint of cider. They were attended by the landlady of the hotel, who, it appears, was not aware that there had been some re-arrangement in the cellar as to the position of the vessels in which the cider and spirits were kept. Some spices or other matter had been put in the cider to correct a tendency to sourness, and this gave it a higher colour, so that Mrs Hayward, who had not been acquainted of the position of the jars, unwittingly supplied a pint of brandy for the cider without detecting any difference in its appearance. The men drank the liquor without making any remark; but it is difficult to believe that, whatever may have been the quality of the brandy, they were not aware that they were drinking something much stronger than cider. At all events, they consumed one pint, and ordered another, which was supplied from the same vessel. When the latter was partially empty, some friend came into the room whom they invited to drink. Immediately upon tasting the liquor he detected what it consisted of and told the men what they were drinking. The second pint was, however, finished, and the two labourers left for their home, apparently not much the worse for the liquor. Nothing more was seen of them until the next morning, when the driver of the mail cart from Chippenham found Robins lying in the road on Tetbury Hill, a few hundred yards from the hotel, in a comatose and insensible state, and 'Bandy', who was more or less stupefied, found himself lying on the road about half a mile from where the deceased was found. The driver of the mail cart proceeded to the house of some persons living near to obtain assistance, but when they returned the unfortunate man was dead. The jury returned a verdict to the effect that the deceased's death resulted from cold and exposure, brought about through indulgence in ardent spirits.

The Tetbury Advertiser

UPPER CAM

THE VILLAGE SCHOOL

The village school stands in a field near the road. There the little mites of children toddle off each morning to acquire the rudiments of learning, such as is deemed necessary to equip them for the struggle with life and circumstance. A few of these are farmer's children; part of them belong to the mechanic or artisan class employed on the railway, or at the distant town, but the majority are the offspring of farm labourers. Some of these dwell in the lanes, some in the fields near at hand, and some at the cottages on the far-away farms. These bring their dinner in little baskets or handkerchiefs, and eat it sitting down under the hedgerows in summer, or in the lobbies or school-room in winter. Sometimes they exchange food with each other – children are fond of tasting each other's bread – or some child living near at hand may invite them to his or her house to eat the viands. When I was a small boy I delighted in exchanging my white bread for that cut from the brown cone wheat loaf of a companion who lived at Owl's Roost Cottages. These children's fare is simple; bread and butter, or lard, jam, or treacle. Sometimes, when you are sitting down to dinner, a timid little rap may come at the door, and, on opening it, some little dot or other will bashfully ask you for a 'dop o' wato'. If you should happen to have a good large mug of lemonade or milk handy, and give him that to drink, holding it to his lips, you will be handsomely repaid with the smile of pleasure and satisfaction which beams on the youngster's physiognomy as he gulps it down, and afterwards requites you for it with a hearty 'tenk-oo'. After this you may be sure the visitor will come again, and bring others as well; but then they never dream of intrusion or imposition; there should be no end to hospitality in their eyes; they have not learned the limitations of life.

  It is a pretty sight to meet the country children coming or going from school; there is much that is exceedingly quaint and picturesque in them, and primitive too. They are bright-looking, fresh and well-kept. Some of the little maids from the farm buildings are very quaint and old-fashioned, in feature, general appearance, and behaviour. They put one in mind of the figures on the old willow-

MINCHINHAMPTON

pattern china-ware. They are not pretty – that is, as is usually understood by prettiness – but by their simplicity of feature and demureness of expression they are exceedingly attractive. Here is no ornament of dressed curls or ribbons, beads, or fine headwear, or frilled frock, or armlet, or dainty brown boots and stockings, gloves or mittens; the child's clothes are plain, simple, and unpretentious, just as you would expect to find them in the circumstances. The face is square, the nose shortish, eyes brown, hair straight, tied over the crown with a piece of old black velvet or braid, dress of drab cloth stuff, print pinafore, dark stockings, and stout, heavy, square-nailed boots, blacked weekly. When it is fine they come unencumbered; if it looks stormy they half carry and half drag a little jacket of coarse material on one side of them. As they near you they lower their eyes and head a little, and partly turn it on one side to avoid your gaze, coyly or timidly, but when they have passed by they will be sure to steal a glance round to see if you are looking at them, and hurry along toward school. Several times, up the lane, they will turn round again to see if you are watching them; nervously if you are a stranger, sociably if you are not. Their parents are poor, and they reflect their comparative poverty; they have not been pampered and spoiled, one can see that; their very bareness and humility force you to sympathize with them. Their cheeks are rosy and firm, the eyes strong and deep, the stature short and stunted, the whole physique hardy and natural, not drawn up like a hot-house plant, and spectacles are very rarely met with in the case of true farm-labourers' offspring.

The boys are of corresponding appearance. They, too, are short in stature – nature always rears a sturdy, hardy plant – generally thick, robust, and well-set. Their hair is usually long and bristly – sticking up for fine weather, as they jokingly say – and home-cut. Their clothes are mostly threadbare, made out of father's left-off, more than likely, often with trousers reaching halfway down the legs, ridiculous to the critical eye of the town-folk. They wear a woollen scarf around the neck in winter, and nothing at all in summer. Their boots are heavy, thick, and cumbersome, and well nailed; such as come from the farms in the fields wear leather gaiters in the winter, and keep them on during the day. The boys will not be as timid and shy as the girls, or not all of them, though the little brothers Gilbert and Jesse were most sensitive in this respect; it was amusing to see their pretty bashfulness,

CHIPPING CAMPDEN

and how they hung their heads and retired behind
the other boys. Bur poor Jesse is dead now; in the
summer a horse in the field kicked the little mite's
brains clean out.

Alfred Williams

THE PIG-MARKET

Part of the High Street was, until a few years since,
called the Pig-Market; for there the inhabitants on
both sides of the way were accustomed, on market
days, to set before their houses pens made of hurdles,
to which pigs were brought for sale. To this offensive
inconvenience they submitted for the poor remunera-
tion of sixpence per day for the use of a pen. At those
times, the high road was so much narrowed that two
carriages could not pass each other.

   While the pig-market was held there, Mr
Saunders, an attorney residing at Lower Grange, a
short distance from the town, had a fancy to fatten
pigs for sale; which he did on an extensive scale, and
taught them to come to their food at the sound of
a bell. Thus it happened, when he had sent a score
of pigs to be sold, and they had been safely penned,

HIGH STREET, STROUD

BURFORD

that Arthur Hewlett, the town crier, rang his bell preparatory to making some public announcement; and the pigs, unable to distinguish one bell from another, no sooner heard Hewlett's than they all leaped over the hurdles, and scampered home to the Grange, in expectation of their food – leaving the pigs of other dealers, as well as the dealers themselves, astonished at the unexpected movement.

Paul Hawkins Fisher

THE SHOEMAKER

The village shoemaker lived in the little stone cottage near the canal, and carried on the trade he had inherited from his father. Formerly he used to make many pairs of boots for the villagers: good, strong, substantial footwear, just the stuff for country places, and especially to wear about the farms in the wet and cold of winter; but this is at an end now. The village cobbler, at any rate, as far as the making of new pairs of boots goes, is very nearly extinct. All the villagers now obtain their clothes and boots from the town – boots at five or six shillings a pair; shoddy cloth trousers, and jackets at a small figure; it is an age of cheapness all round. The boots are worn out in a short while, and the clothes, too. A few soakings with wet betray the former: they drop all to pieces when placed before the fire to dry; and you come in contact with the slightest projection, or strain your trousers or coat, the falsely-woven fabric rips and tears, and might easily put you in a quandary. A good pair of men's boots, made of best leather by the village shoemaker – 'bucks', as they were called, from the old fellow's nickname – cost sixteen or eighteen shillings. When we were small boys and went to school ours cost eight shillings and sixpence, as I remember, and were securely water-tight. This we soon ascertained, because we made haste to try them in the first ditch or pool we came to.

The shoemaker and his wife lived happily enough together, though he was often harsh and unfeeling towards her, and called her 'an old fool', and shouted at her at the top of his voice, and spoke of her

NORTHLEACH

to everyone as 'my ow 'ooman'; but she bore it all very patiently, and nodded and smiled, and winked now and then, and shed a few tears, and was most slavish in her attendance on him, denying herself the necessaries of life to procure things for his comfort, though she was nearly broken-hearted at the end, for he fell ill with cancer, and because of her deafness would not have her at the bedside, but motioned with his arms, and told the others to keep her away; he didn't want her there. After her husband died she continued in the cottage a little while on parish pay, and finally went to the workhouse, where she died at eighty. In her young days, as a girl, she worked about the fields for the farmer, minding the pigs and sheep, and received a piece of bacon in weekly payment. If everyone had as kind a heart as the old shoemaker's wife, how much better a great many of us would be, and the world about us as well!

Alfred Williams

THE AMATEUR TORY

I shall never forget a meeting held at Northleach a few years ago. It was at a time when the balance of parties was so even that our Unionist member was returned by the bare majority of three votes, only to be unseated a few weeks afterwards on a recount. Northleach is a very Radical town, about six miles from my home; and when I agreed to take the chair, I little knew what an unpleasant job I had taken in hand. Our member for some reason or other was unable to attend, I therefore found myself at 7.30 one evening facing two hundred 'red-hot' Radicals, with only one other speaker besides myself to keep the ball a-rolling. My companion was one of those professional politicians of the baser sort, who call themselves Unionists because it pays better for the working-class politician – in just the same way as ambitious young men among the upper classes sometimes become Radicals on the strength of there being more opening for them on the 'Liberal' side.

Well, this fellow bellowed away in the usual ranting style for about three-quarters of an hour; his eloquence was great, but truth was 'more honoured in the breach than in the observance'. So that when

GREAT BARRINGTON

he sat down, and my turn came, the audience, instead of being convinced, was fairly rabid. I was very young at that time, and fearfully nervous; added to which I was never much of a speaker, and, if interrupted at all, usually lost the thread of my argument.

After a bit they began shouting, 'Speak up.' The more they shouted the more mixed I got. When once the spirit of insubordination is roused in these fellows, it spreads like wildfire. The din became so great I could not hear myself speak. In about five minutes there would have been a row. Suddenly a bright idea occurred to me. 'Listen to me,' I shouted; 'as you won't hear me speak, perhaps you would allow me to sing you a song.' I had a fairly strong voice, and could go up a good height; so I gave them 'Tom Bowling'. Directly I started you could have heard a pin drop. They gave me a fair hearing all through; and when, as a final climax, I finished up with a prolonged B flat – a very loud and long note, which sounded to me something between a 'view holloa'; and the whistle of a penny steamboat, but which came in nicely as a sort of *pièce de résistance*, fairly astonishing 'Hodge' – their enthusiasm knew no bounds. They cheered and cheered again. Hand shaking went on all round, whilst the biggest Radical of the lot stood up and shouted, 'You be a little Liberal, I know, and the other blokes 'ave 'ired you.'

J. Arthur Gibbs

THE WOOD SALE

'Holloa, Daniel!' I said to a labourer, 'how did the wood sale go off yesterday?'

'Oh! 'twere a puffec' sale, sir, a puffec' sale! Thur wur just as much drink a-gwine as a chap wur a minded to he'. 'Twurn't no nasty stuff nether, but good, honest drink as 'ad a-got summat in't, yer knaow, an' made a man knaow soonish as he wur a-getting nicely forrud. Willum an' I, us went up thur together, an' when's got thur, thur wur th' owld squire a-stood outside a-telling on 'um to bring this 'ere drink up, an' to let the folks get it into 'um fast as iver they wur a-minded. "Twun't hurt 'ee," er said,

MORETON-IN-MARSH

"twun't hurt 'ee, 'tis some good wholesome tack," er said; "'tis some reubub weind as I've a-had by me this ten year, an' it's only gone off a mossel; it's good stuff for 'ee," er says, a-tossing off a glass as keind like as cud be. Wail, they brings up this 'ere licker in great warter cans, an' one on 'em says to I, "Will 'ee drenk?" "Sure as life I 'ull," I says.

"Yer won't git such tack as this yere agen," er says, "thur's a bit of a querish taste to't," er says, "but yer'll soon git used to that. It's a rare powerful drink," er says, "an' will warm 'ee up a rum un," er says, a-handing we a third lot on't. Wall, 'ee wur right enow about it. 'Twer querish tack, sommat like beer an reubub weind an' bacca-juice a-mixed, but I knowed we could git forrud on't, an' 'twur stuff as warmed a body right down to ers toes. Owld Job Smith got as drunk as a genelman on't, an' as blind as a 'oont, er couldn't see whur er wur a-gwine, an' veil yead furst into a faggit-pile.

"Does 'ee zell th' owld genelman long o this lot?" says one.

"'Twould spile it if yer did," says another. "'Twould cost too much in vind the skeandalous owld twoad wi' licker;" and he as sed it wur on's back afore we'd got much further.

'All the way as us went the folks kept a-drapping off one by one. Some on 'em had a-bought their bit most skeandalous dear; but then that wur wot thic tack wur a-sard out fur. 'Twoodn't never a-payed 'em else to perwide it. Owld Wilium wur luckier nor I, somehow. He got a skinful afore I cud. Time was when Wilium and I cud set down together with the mug atween us, and we was so ekal as none cud tell the one on us as wur forruder nor t'other. But this 'ere time I'd a 'd to leave Willum a-hind, and, yer knaow, when us corned to the last lot the licker had a-knocked the company all abroad, so as thur wurn't nun on-us beseps th' auctioneer, an's clerk, and mysel' around un. True as I be 'ere, that thur's true, measter. I'll teak my sollum Davy on't. Yer cud look back and see all along and atween and atwixt the losts the yolks a-lying and a-sprawlin' about the ground wur they'd a-bin auvercum wi' that thur tack of the squire's. Ah,' he said, smacking his lips, 'it wur proper powerful tack, thur's no doubt on't.'

"Wall," the auctioneer says, says 'ee, "who's a-gwine to bid fur this 'ere lot?"

"Seems to I, sur," I sed, "as thur ain't much choice fur 'ee. Thur ain't a gurt sight of comp'ny around

NORTHLEACH

'ee. You've a-bin a bit too quick-like for 'em thease time. Then yolk o' the squire's had ought to a-bin a bit mussiful on 'em till you'd a-finished."

"Strike me, Dan'l," er said, "we've a-done some business to-day. I've a-knocked down all the folks as well as all the lots."

'I thowt about as how I best be a-getting whoam, so I goes and finds Willum a-leaning agin the faggit-stack; and putting my earn into hissen we makes our way – and a middlingish crukked way 'twere, I tell 'ee – into the road. Soon's ever we'd a-got upon 't, "Dan'l," er said, "this 'ere road's a-running away from under I like a mad thing," and down we went on ers back arl a-mullock in the middle on't. "Dan'l," er sed, a-setting up, "wi'm nought else to do but to sot down yere-right, and let this 'ere road take we straight whoam, ers muving hard thuc way."

"No er ain't, Willum," I says, "er ain't a-muving, thee'lt nivir git whoam to-night ef thee doesn't muv theeself."

"Muv mese Dan'l!" er said, "d'ye think I'm sich a fule as to walk when I can ride whoam free and fur nowt? I'se gwine whoam just like a genelman. Set down, Dan'l, do."

'Wall, sum'ow I comed down just beside un, and dratted if I didn't seem to see the road a-running away wi' us, only it sim to I as if er wur a-gwine round and round 'stead of strait vorruds. So there us two sot in the middle of the road, wi' our fit stuck out in front on's, and let that thur road take us whur er was a-minded.

"Howld fast, Dan'l," says Willum, "Lord, how the thing do go! Look 'ow the trees do vly be we, Dan'l."

"Willum," I says to un, quiet like, "Willum," I says, "how d'ye think ye'll stop the plaguey thing when yer comes anent the door?"

'"Why, I'll cry whoa, in course, Dan'l," er says.

"Cry whoa! will 'ee? D'ye thenk as this 'ere road's a-gwine to stop for you a-crying whoa? If

BISLEY

er should we'd best cry whoa! now, fur seems to I as er's a-gwine round and round, and us ain't a mossel nigher."

"Lord, Dan'l, if er 'oont stop we'll be carried right into the tound. I'll cry whoa!" says 'ee, and then er set to and hollered – but the theng 'ouldn't stop. "Darze your little back on 'ee, yer plaguey twoad! Whoa! can't 'ee."

"Willum," I says, "strikes me we'ed best holloa whoa! together. 'Tis but nat'ral as a road is summat hard o' yerring."

"Right you be, Dan'!," er says, "so look 'ee 'ere; when I says dree we'll holler whoa together. One! two! thee!" And wi' that we hollered whoa! loud enow to stop a dozen teams o' 'osses; but it hadn't no effec' on that thur road, er went off harder nor iver. Just then a young feller cum up to we.

"What the deuce," er says, "be you two vules a-setting thur side by side in the middle o' the road fur?"

"Why, thease 'ere road," says Willum, "have a-run'd away o' we, and us can't stop un nohow. We've a-hollered all we knowed."

"Runned away with 'ee! it's the drink as 'ave runned away wi' yer heads, and as fur hollering," er said, "yer've hollered wuss nor a pair of bulls. I cudn't thenk wot the world had a-auvertook 'ee. But git up aff thease here road or you'll be run'd auver."

"Wall, stop un, first," says Willum.

"Stop un, you drunken yule!" er says, "stop un! why, er ain't a-muving. Git up with 'ee."

'Wall, I puts my hand on Willum's showlder to see if I cowd git up arra ways, but just as I wur half-ways, Willum, he catched hoult of my leg to try and pull hisself up, and down we two come agin in the road; and thur we was a-trying, fust one and then t'other on us, to git up by a-leaning one on t'other, and all we did was to vail about in the road while thic chap stood by and laffed fit to bust hisseif. Bimeby Willum says, says 'ee, "Dan'l," er says, "tain't nere a mossel o' use a-trying to wark on a toad as is a-running away from under 'ee an the time; let's crawl quietly on to the sward at the zide."

'And so us did; us set to and crawled on our hands 'cross the road till us got on to the grass, true as I be here; but us couldn't neither on us stan' then, so us had to lie down theer-right and bide.'

S.S. Buckman

EVIDENCE FOR THE INSPECTOR

Mary Peart, of Kilcot, a hamlet in the parish of Newent, Gloucestershire; husband aged 47; works for Mr Hooper; earns 9s. or 10s. a week. Has five children at home, aged respectively 12, 10, 7, 4 and 1 years; none of them earns anything, but she is trying to get the eldest (a girl) out to service. Requires 3 pecks of flour a week for the consumption of the family; flour is now selling at 1 s. 6d. a bushel. Has no vegetables, not so much as a potato left. Has had nothing but 'stark-naked bread', this month past; no butter, cheese, or bacon. Has had no cheese since harvest. Sometimes even the bread runs very short; has been two or three days without knowing where to turn for a bit. The rent of her cottage, which contains two rooms on the ground floor, and two small bedchambers, with a garden about 30 perches, is £5, besides rates, which come to about 15s. more. It is a good, comfortable house, but the rent is too high for a labouring man to pay. Her husband is a steady man, and brings his money home.

(Note: The Revd Morris Burland, who was present when I took this evidence, informed me that in his district, containing about 400 houses, there must be at least 50 families as badly off as this. I certainly hardly ever saw a district with more marks of poverty about it; many of the cottages ruinous, and unfit for human habitation; a low wage-rate, and a correspondingly low social and intellectual condition of the people; a great number of apparently truant children; a great aversion on the part of some of the worst-housed old people to take refuge in the workhouse, though they would be infinitely more comfortable there. The most wretched dens that I saw inhabited were such as had been erected by squatters on the waste; but there were others . . . not many degrees better in condition, for which rent . . . as high as £3 11s. (per annum) is paid.–January 28, 1868.)

Revd F. Fraser. First Report of the Royal Commission on the Employment of Children

ASLEEP IN THE PIG CART

At Stroud County Court on Wednesday, the case of Harvey versus King was tried. The plaintiff is supervisor of excise at Stroud, and he was driving home from Tetbury one night last month, and when near Nailsworth, at an angle of the road, he drove against the defendant's pig cart which was on the wrong side, and the driver of which was asleep, by which he sustained an accident. He brought his action to recover damages, £7 10s., for the actual injury done to the gig and harness, and for the medical attendance, and judgement was given for the plaintiff for the full amount.

Wilts. & Glos. Standard

MR BONTHRON'S HOLIDAY

'All clear ahead?'

'Ay, ay, sir,' responded the chief mate, giving the starting handle a turn and letting go the painter, in compliance with further commands. So now we're off at last on our long-talked-of canal cruise through the heart of England in our 6 h.p. Daimler.

The run to Lechlade was quite satisfactory, with very interesting navigation, owing to the tortuous character of the Thames the whole way. The country all up this part, although not striking in scenery, is of a delightfully rural nature. During this part of the journey we had continuously showery weather; however, being well protected on board with a top awning, and another sheet round aft, it in no way affected our pleasure, or even dampened our spirits.

Lechlade we duly reached about 8.30 p.m., having caught some fine glimpses of Thames scenery. The venerable landlord of eighty-four summers of the Trout Inn was waiting to receive us, and we

ST JOHN'S LOCK, LECHLADE

stayed for the night at this quaint little place.

The Thames and Severn Canal, like most others, has had a varied career, and has consequently not developed as perhaps it might. The report about the condition of the weeds there again was such that we re-engaged our horseman, 'John Gilpin', who not only stood by, but did yeoman service in pulling us through the parts where the propeller refused to go round, and glad we were of the auxiliary assistance.

We passed Kempsford and Cricklade and eventually reached Cirencester by a cutting about one-and-a-half miles from the main canal, and at this point we had to break our journey and leave the boat, owing to the repairs to the canals. From there we all hied back to town by rail, quite pleased with our trip and experiences so far. Cirencester is a typical English market town of considerable antiquity.

Travelling down from London on the following Friday night to Cirencester with our party of five all told, we resumed our journey on the Thames and Severn Canal, making an early start next morning, as we had a heavy day's work before us. The weather broke badly at our start, but cleared up afterwards very fine; but we were rather pleased at this, as the Thames and Severn water was not

THE TROUT INN, LECHLADE

DANEWAY BRIDGE

then over-abundant on the summit. After what we had come through with weeds, etc., we again had a horse and man provided, so as not to lose any time, and we were towed right to Sapperton Tunnel, some seven miles on.

This Sapperton is a fine piece of tunnelling, and, I understand, one of the longest in England, being two-and-a-quarter miles in length. It was built at the end of the eighteenth century. Our intention was to motor through, but with the engine racing a little, and with patches of weeds here and there in the tunnel (although the water is comparatively clear) we decided to work the boat through. This we did by the aid of our boathooks and a wire running along the side. We eventually accomplished this rather exciting piece of work in one hour and thirty-five minutes – all hands being at work. Both at the entrance to the tunnel and at the exit the rural scenery is very striking.

After this the lock work begins seriously from the summit at Daneway, with group after group of locks, there being twenty-eight for the remaining seven miles to Wallbridge, Stroud, and this took us from 2.15 p.m. up till half-past eight. The scenery on the latter run is of the finest description: one has the splendid advantage of seeing what is known

SAPPERTON TUNNEL ENTRANCE

THE THAMES NEAR KEMPSFORD

CERNEY LOCK

WHARF COTTAGE, DANEWAY

as the Golden Valley to the fullest extent. As one wends one's way down the scenic effects are very fine indeed; in fact, this part of the trip amply repaid us for any tediousness there was in coming through the multitudinous locks, which are so slow in filling. After the tunnel, our motor, working well, was brought into requisition, and we continued with it right through from there. We had the service of lock-keepers nearly all the way down, or got assistance, otherwise it would have entailed a heavy day's work. We were rather unfortunate with our locks here, in so far that a barge was ahead of us and the locks were against us all the way through. In consequence of this, our day's run was curtailed by, say, a couple of hours, but one must accept the inevitable in canal life. As before mentioned, we duly reached Wallbridge, Stroud, the end of the Thames and Severn Canal.

P. Bonthron

ON BOARD THE FLOWER OF GLOSTER

Soon after Chalford the grey houses with their blue slate roofs grow fewer in number, the hills at each side become higher; there are broader pasture fields;

MR BONTHRON'S *BALGONIE*

THE THAMES & SEVERN CANAL AT CHALFORD

a stray farm or a lock-house is all you can see of human habitation. In the nearer distance the dense woods spread over the rolling land and, like an army in glittering mail, with golden trappings and with coloured plumes, they march down the hillsides to the water's edge.

This part of the country must be the most luxurious in the whole of England. In the half-hour's ramble through these woods while Eynsham Harry was preparing the midday meal I counted seventeen various sorts of wild flowers then in bloom. There were bluebells and orchis – those deep-red purple orchis with their spotted leaves which, in the midst of the dark violet of the bluebells, made such colours as they wore in the great days of Rome's Empire. Could the imperial toga have been indeed as imperial as these?

I found the cuckoo-pint as well, its livid finger in that pale fragile sheath of green. There were nettles, red and white, but with such bloom as would shame many a hot-house plant in London. Veronica was there, with its tiny blossoms that might match the cobalt of any Chinese dynasty you liked to name. Garlic I found, and primroses hiding from the heat of May, the last I knew that I should see that year. The violets grew so thickly, I could scarce but tread them down. Ground ivy crawled in every open space and, with roots dripping in the cool water, there were forget-me-nots, king-cups with blossoms of metallic gold and lesser celandine, apeing the glories of their sovereign.

I found strawberries in blossom and the purple flowers of common bugle. There was herb-robert with its brilliant scented leaf, stitchwort and salvia. I have no doubt I missed a great many more. There must have been knotted figwort, there must have

CHALFORD

View at Chalford.

CHALFORD

been white and purple comfrey. I saw no plants of willow herb, yet they must have been there as well. But I had no time to count them all, their abundance was so overwhelming.

And with all these jewelled flowers, imagine a valley of gold. The leaves of the countless trees all set before you in the golden flush of youth; the fields upon the other bank dipped in the gold of a myriad buttercups and cowslips; the sunlight streaming on it all from a cloudless sky in May – gold – all gold – a priceless valley paved in gold and precious stones.

When I came out from the shadows of those woods into the sunshine again I could only stand and wonder, wonder what any man would say – his first words – if on a magic carpet I could whip him up from the grey streets and plant him there where I stood. It would probably be something in the nature of blasphemy, but acceptable nevertheless to the God who made it all – far more acceptable as a genuine need of praise than any prayer of thanksgiving grudgingly offered in a consecrated church.

I returned silently to the barge; as silently sat down to my midday meal. Presently I became conscious of the fact that Eynsham Harry was watching me while I eat.

"What is it?' I asked.

'I be waiting for you to taste that dish, sur,' said he. It was a dish of green vegetable, looking as much like spinach as anything else. I thought it was spinach.

'Where did you get it?' I enquired.

'Would you be so good as to just taste it, sur,' he repeated.

I obeyed, looking up at him as I did so with that pensive expression when you specialise. It is part of your uniform, whether it be in the tea factory, the pulpit, or the house of parliament. All specialists are actors.

'Tastes like asparagus,' said I. 'Where did you get it from?'

Still he would not tell me. 'You like it, sur?' he persisted. I tried another mouthful. 'It's better than asparagus,' said I. 'Put a little pepper wi' it, sur.' I put a little pepper and tasted again.

'By Jove,' said I, 'it's damned good! Where did you get it?'

He pointed to a line of hedge half-way up the hill.

'There be hops growing up on that hedge, sur,' said he; 'these that you're eating be the young shoots,

BUSSAGE

cut off about six inches from the top and boiled the same as other greens. In the month of May we takes 'en whenever we can. The wilder the better.'

For more than three miles the canal divides the wooded hills, a band of silver drawn through this valley of gold. Lock by lock it mounts the gentle incline until it reaches the pound to Sapperton Tunnel, and at the summit spreads into a wide basin before it passes into the last lock, some few hundred yards before the tunnel's mouth.

The whole way from Stroud upwards is almost deserted now. We only met one barge in the whole journey. An old lady with a capacious barge bonnet was standing humming quietly to herself at the tiller. That was the only boat we found on those waters. The locks are, however, good; some of them have only just been made within the last few years. But the draught of water is bad; in some places we just floated, and no more. It was stern work for our horse Fanny then. There were times when I thought the tow-line must give way, the strain upon it was so great.

In one short pound more shallow than the rest, we came upon two little boys bathing. One swimming manfully, making great pace and great commotion, struggling as though for dear life; while the other, knee-deep in the shallow water, stood by in undisguised admiration. I strongly suspect the swimmer had one leg upon the bottom. I could always swim so well like that myself. I know too how splendid it looks, for if you make a splash enough not a soul can see.

After our meal we went on through the rest of this wonderful valley. It was golden to the last. Even in the water itself the weeds grew more luxuriantly than I have seen in any river. In and out of the forests of trailing weed the fish moved mysteriously, like mermaids in a fairy tale. It was all a fairy tale beneath that water. There were dense growths, and then clear spaces on to which the sunshine fell in brilliant patches. The pen of Hans Andersen could have found many a story in the magic country beneath the still water of the canal.

At the top of the valley, looking down between the hills through a lattice-work of apple blossom,

DANEWAY BASIN, AND WHARF COTTAGE

stands the Bricklayers Arms, a little inn with two or three houses clustered round it. An old man there described to me the opening of the tunnel in the reign of George III. He had not seen it himself.

'My big grandfather' – this was how he told it to me – 'my big grandfather, the day the tunnel was opened, he was walking down the tow-path, and he met a feller coming along, and he said to my big grandfather, "Where are you going, my man?"

"I'm going to see the king," he says.

"I am the king," says the man, and gives him a guinea; and when he looks at the head on the coin, I'm dommed if it worn't.'

It was rather nice, that little touch of human incredulity. I can see him comparing the likeness with that of the head on the coin, catching the face in profile before he finally made up his mind that he was being told the truth.

The passage through that tunnel of Sapperton, which, on a sudden bend of the canal, opens a deep black mouth into the heart of the hills, was the only time when the voyage of the *Flower of Gloster* has in the sense of stirring adventure. Into the grim darkness you glide and, within half an hour, are lost in a lightless cavern where the drip, drip of the clammy water sounds incessantly in your ears.

Some time ago, when there was more constant traffic on this canal, there were professional leggers to carry you through; for there is no tow-path, and the barge must be propelled by the feet upon the side walls of the tunnel. Now that the barges pass so seldom, this profession has become obsolete. There are no leggers. For four hours Eynsham Harry and I lay upon our sides on the wings that are fitted to the boat for that purpose, and legged every inch of the two and three-quarter miles. It was not a gentle job. Countless were the number of times I looked on ahead to that faint pin-point of light; but by such infinite degrees did it grow larger as we neared the end, that I thought we should never reach it.

"What used the leggers to be paid?' I asked after the first mile, when it seemed all sensation had gone out of my limbs and they were working merely in obedience to the despairing effort of my will.

'Five shillings, sir, for a loaded boat. Two and six for an empty one.' I groaned.

'A pound wouldn't satisfy me,' said I.

THE BRICKLAYERS ARMS, DANEWAY

SAPPERTON TUNNEL ENTRANCE NEAR DANEWAY

OAKRIDGE

'No, sur, I suspects not. It's always easier to do these things for nothing.'

For an hour that was all we said. For an hour I legged away, thinking how true that casual statement was – 'It's always easier to do these things for nothing.' It is – always. All labour would be play were it not for payment. The man who reckons is worse than lost, he is made; than which there can be no more bitter a punishment. Once, then, the labourer is paid, he begins a-reckoning of his hire, and that is all. From this come revolution and anarchy.

But one does not think of this sort of thing for long while legging it through Sapperton Tunnel. A drip of shiny water on one's face is quite enough to upset the most engrossing contemplation. I saw the pin-point of light growing to the pin's head, and still we laboured on, only resting a few moments to light a fresh piece of candle or take breath.

It was evening when we came out into the light again and, though the sun had set, with shadows falling everywhere, it almost dazzled me. A barge in the next lock rose above the lock's arms, with every line cut out against the pale sky.

E. Temple Thurston

GRANNIES

Granny Trill and Granny Wallon were rival ancients and lived on each other's nerves, and their perpetual enmity was like mice in the walls and absorbed much of my early days. With their sickle-bent bodies, pale pink eyes, and wild wisps of hedgerow hair, they looked to me the very images of witches and they were also much alike. In all their time as close neighbours they never exchanged a word. They communicated instead by means of boots and brooms – jumping on floors and knocking on ceilings. They referred to each other as "Er-Down-Under' and "Er-Up-Atop, the Varmint'; for each to the other was an airy nothing, a local habitation not fit to be named.

'Er-Down-Under, who lived on our level, was perhaps the smaller of the two, a tiny white shrew who came nibbling through her garden, who clawed squeaking with gossip at our kitchen window, or

NEAR OAKRIDGE

sat sucking bread in the sun; always mysterious and self-contained and feather-soft in her movements. She had two names, which she changed at will according to the mood of her day. Granny Wallon was her best, and stemmed, we were told, from some distinguished alliance of the past. Behind this crisp and trotting body were certainly rumours of noble blood. But she never spoke of them herself. She was known to have raised a score of children. And she was known to be very poor. She lived on cabbage, bread, and potatoes—but she also made excellent wines.

Granny Wallon's wines were famous in the village, and she spent a large part of her year preparing them. The gathering of the ingredients was the first of the mysteries. At the beginning of April she would go off with her baskets and work round the fields and hedges, and every fine day till the end of the summer would find her somewhere in the evening, bearing her cargoes of crusted flowers, till she had buckets of cowslips, dandelions, elder-blossom crammed into every corner of the house. The elder-flower, drying on her kitchen floor, seemed to cover it with a rancid carpet, a crumbling rime of grey-green blossom fading fast in a dust of summer. Later the tiny grape-cluster of the elderberry itself would be seething in purple vats, with daisies and orchids thrown in to join it, even strands of the dog-rose bush.

What seasons fermented in Granny Wallon's kitchen, what summers were brought to the boil, with limp flower-heads piled around the floor holding fast to their clotted juices – the sharp spiced honey of those cowslips first, then the coppery reeking dandelion, the bitter poppy's whiff of powder, the cat's-breath, death-green elder. Gleanings of days and a dozen pastures, strippings of lanes and hedges – she bore them home to her flag-tiled kitchen, sorted them each from each, built up her fires and loaded her pots, and added her sugar and yeast. The vats boiled daily in suds of sugar, revolving petals in throbbing water, while the air, aromatic, steamy, embalmed, distilled the hot dews and flowerly soups and ran the wine down the dripping walls.

And not only flower-heads went into these brews; the old lady used parsnips, too, potatoes, sloes, crab-apples, quinces, in fact anything she could lay her hands on. Granny Wallon made wine as though

OAKRIDGE

demented, out of anything at all; and no doubt, if given enough sugar and yeast, could have made a drink out of a box of old matches.

She never hurried or hoarded her wines, but led them gently through their natural stages. After the boiling they were allowed to settle and to work in the cool of the vats. For several months, using pieces of toast, she scooped off their yeasty sediments. Then she bottled and labelled each liquor in turn and put them away for a year.

At last one was ready, then came the day of distribution. A squeak and a rattle would shake our window, and we'd see the old lady, wispily grinning, waving a large white jug in her hand.

'Hey there, missus! Try this'n, then. It's the first of my last year's cowslips.'

Through the kitchen window she'd fill up our cups and watch us, head cocked, while we drank. The wine in the cups was still and golden, transparent as a pale spring morning. It smelt of ripe grass in some far-away field and its taste was as delicate as air. It seemed so innocent, we would swig away happily and even the youngest guzzled it down. Then a curious rocking would seize the head; tides rose from our feet like a fever, the kitchen walls began to shudder and shift, and we all fell in love with each other.

Very soon we'd be wedged, tight-crammed, in the window, waving our cups for more, while our Mother, bright-eyed, would be mumbling gaily: 'Lord bless you, Granny. Fancy cowsnips and parsney. You must give me the receipt, my dear.'

Granny Wallon would empty the jug in our cups, shake out the last drops on the flowers, then trot off tittering down the garden path, leaving us hugging ourselves in the window.

Laurie Lee

THOMAS AND JANE

In a cottage opposite a farmyard dwell old Thomas and Jane – the Darby and Joan of the Thames-side – who, though both within one year of a century, retain an active and intelligent interest in the life and

LAVERTON

work of the village, and especially in the threshing, which they can view sitting before their cottage window. Very different indeed are things now from what they were when these two were first wed. They have seen generations come and go and have outlived their own time, till they have become strangers to the village in which they were born and to the scenes amid which they have so long dwelt.

Ninety-three years is a long time for a mortal to remember a thing, yet old Thomas's memory extends back so far. 'When he was six years of age he used to run into the farmyard to watch the men at work with the oxen and horses. One day, in the presence of old farmer Archer, the men were trying to yoke a big bull to a manure cart, but, try as they might, the animal would not back into the desired position. At last young Tom became impatient and, to the amazement of the men and the delight of the farmer, cried:

'Let I 'ev a try, an' see if I can wutt un in.' The farmer smiled at the youngster and exclaimed: 'Go on! Let the child try.'

Accordingly, young Tom, who was so tiny that a good snort of the beast might have knocked him down, took the halter, cried 'Wutt back!' to the bull, and backed it into the shafts very simply and easily. Then old Archer laughed heartily at the youngster and told him to come into the stalls, and thereupon appointed him master of the bull and gave him three shillings a week in wages, which was double the amount received by the other boys who were older than he.

After that he took the oxen to plough, learned to sow, reap, and thresh, and performed the hundred and one duties of the farm. His wife's father was a maker of baskets and sieves for winnowing the corn in the barn after hand-threshing, and her mother was a lace-maker at a time when the cottage industries had not entirely disappeared from the region. A family of twelve followed their marriage; they have between two and three hundred grandchildren and great-grandchildren, and several sons who are in receipt of the old-age pension.

Of the two, granny is the more active and energetic. Clad in an old, faded gown, with woollen vest, a pair of knitted stockings, with feet cut off, drawn up the arms, and quaint little cap on the head, she hops to and fro with surprising agility, cleans the grate, sweeps up the floor, dusts the ornaments and pictures, and sees to her housework generally, while the old man grips his fork or spade and toils in the garden among the potatoes and cauliflowers. 'I got a goodish spirit an' tha's what kips I up,' says granny, while Thomas smiles approvingly, reaches his pipe, half burnt away, from the mantelpiece, fills it with tobacco, and lights it with a spill from the hob.

'I got to master'n now, same as 'e allus 'ed,' granny says, with a triumphant little laugh and a knowing wag of the head, at the same time giving her husband a playful cuff. Gramp wears an old pair of trousers with patches half a yard long over each knee, a thick woollen overall, and a little brown felt hat, which he keeps on his head indoors and out.

Their daily mode of living and general routine are as follows: Rise at 7a.m., breakfast at 8; dinner – a little meat, broth, bread, and potatoes – at noon; tea at 3.30; supper at 6, and retire at 7p.m. Granny's breakfast consists of a basin of bread and water sops with a lump of butter and a little salt and pepper added. This she prepares every afternoon ready to heat in the saucepan the following morning. For supper she takes a cup of warm beer with bread; to this habit she attributes her long life and good health. Years ago they lived principally on butter, milk, and 'skim dick,' i.e. cheese made of skimmed milk, which form of diet may have been the cause of their attaining to such a great age. Old Thomas says they never felt the need of butcher's meat – it made them sick to eat it.

Every Saturday the big living-room in the cottage is subjected to an extra special turn out. The tables and chairs are moved aside, and granny, provided with pail, brush, and house-cloth, scrubs the stone floor and then whitens it with freestone, rubbing it round and round and describing many curious and fantastical figures that resemble a child's first exercise in calligraphy. This is performed early in the morning, before breakfast; then grandfather has to lie in bed an hour later so as not to obstruct the most important operation of all the week.

'Afore I married 'e,' says granny, 'I used to help missis in the dairy. I can remember 't as well as ef 'twas but isterdi. Maaster used to go to church every wik, an' one Sunday marnin', when us was all set at dinner, a turned to I an' sed:

"Byen you well today, Jane?"

"Yes, I be all right," I sed.

"Cos thaay bin talkin' about you in church."

"An' a good job too! I don' keer what tha dons," I sed to 'n.'

This was when the banns were published. Afterwards master and mistress subscribed and bought her a wedding gown, and made them a present of a side of bacon and a cheese that the cunning little mice had nibbled slightly with their pretty teeth.

Alfred Williams

THE LARGE WEDDING

I heard a discussion in a bankruptcy court in the Midlands, a few weeks ago, as to where Stow-on-the-Wold was. Only two persons in court seemed to know its 'locale'. The official receiver said he did, and another gentleman told an official that it would take him two days to get there!

Well, even Stow has its notable events. On the 12th ult., a wedding was to have taken place in this small town perched high up on the Cotswolds, but when the happy couple, with a considerable number of admiring friends, arrived at the parish church at the appointed time, no clergyman was present. The minutes dragged on, and as he did not arrive a search was made for him, but without effect. After an hour had elapsed, a sturdy farmer went into the belfry, and began tolling the bell, in the hope of attracting the attention of the rector if he was within earshot. It happened, however, that for many years the church bell had been used to alarm the town whenever there was a fire, and so when the inhabitants heard it tolling at such an unusual hour, they concluded that there was a 'blaze' somewhere. A scene of excitement followed. Numbers ran towards the church to find out where the fire was, and the

STOW-ON-THE-WOLD

fire brigade hastily assembled, mounted the fire engine, and drove at rapid rate to the church. When the sensation was at its height, the rector came running up. He breathlessly explained that he had entirely forgotten about the wedding, and the couple were finally married in the presence of a far larger gathering than they had anticipated.

The Tetbury Advertiser

REYNARD

The following anecdote of the sagacity of a fox, which was witnessed here [Green], was told me by the late Miss Dimock of Stonehouse. Her father was a clothier residing at Bridgend, in the Stonehouse valley, near the village of that name; and a workman at his factory, who lived at Harescombe, passed across the Green to and from his work, daily. Early one morning, as he was on his way, he saw in the obscure light some animal stealing along, and apparently with a heavy load. His curiosity being excited, he followed, and soon perceived that it was a fox carrying a goose toward the wood which crowns the hill above Standish Park. He saw the fox attempt several times to leap over the wall into the wood, with the goose in his mouth, but its weight as often pulled him back. He then placed the goose close to the wall, leaped on it, and, stretching forward, tried to reach his prey as it lay on the ground. In this, too, he failed. But the wall was what is called a dry wall, and built of rough, unhewn stones without mortar; and the fox leaped down, and after a short seeming deliberation, seized the head of the goose, and thrust its long bill into a crevice of the wall, as high up in it as he could reach; then mounting again, he drew it from the wall, dragged the goose over into the wood, and was gone.

Paul Hawkins Fisher

CHILDHOOD AT THE RIDGE

My twin sister and I were born at The Ridge on the 23rd of October 1869. Except for a boy, born three years later, we were the youngest of a family of six boys and four girls. There is a most beautiful view

THE RIDGE

from the windows of the room in which we first opened our eyes – the glorious woods beyond the park, the Vale below them, the silver Severn, and the soft blue Welsh and Malvern Hills.

Of that room I have recollections how we used to go there every morning for our Bible reading with Mother. We learnt a great deal of the Bible by heart and I still have one, given me when seven years old by my elder sisters, at the end of which Mother wrote 'Maggie knows . . .' followed by a list of the passages we had learnt.

Below the windows of the room a wide terrace, on which opened the library, drawing-room and dining-room, ran the length of the house and along the back of the conservatory. Below it were two tennis-courts with steps down to each – the lower one being divided from the park by a ha-ha. The front of the conservatory formed one side of a large garden, with ribbon borders planted in the fashion of those days with such brilliant flowers as geraniums, lobelia, ageratum and calceolarias. On to this garden looked the quarters of us children, bedrooms, nurseries, schoolrooms, as well as my father's study and the smoking-room for the big boys.

THE TWIN BENGOUGH SISTERS

A TRIP FROM HOME

The front of the house was very pillared and porticoed, and on either side of the steps was a large pleasant-faced lion couchant, made of stone. They were great pets of us children; being large enough for three or four of us to ride on at once. Another fascination there, neatly hidden in the house wall, was a tiny square hole with a wooden door – a most suitable home for a goblin – but its real use was a receptacle for a little paper proof that a policeman had been round in the night to look after us.

To the stable yard on half holidays we three would repair, and Vizard, the kind coachman, would pretent to bring out our make believe horses 'Juggler', 'Ladislas', and 'Snowball', on which, with the help of a little imagination, we would ride down to Waterley Bottom, calling at the cottages of our particular friends. First to dear old white-haired Timothy French, who would greet us with 'Will 'ee 'ave an opple? 'Ave a drop o' zyder-r?' Gratefully accepting the 'opple' but not the 'zyder-r', our next visit w to Mrs Wilkins and her daughter Ann, where we would be regaled with bread and rhubarb jam. Then up to the little Ridge chapel, near to which in one of the cottages lived kind Mrs Park, the wife of one of the gardeners – whose excellent ginger beer we much enjoyed. And so home singing at the top of our young voices. We were all very fond of music, and the story goes that once, after a children's party at the house of my godfather, Mr Forbes [Grange, Uley], we twins, then aged about three, were found singing 'Rule Britannia' to a no doubt admiring audience in the servants' hall.

To go back to Vizard, the coachman. He made us a rhyme about the horses, which ran as follows:

Peter, Perfection, Paddy and Punch
All paid a visit to old Mother Bunch.
But Mother Bunch was talking to Charley
Over a bin of oats and barley.

'Mother Bunch' and 'Charley' were the carriage pair, and the others, except 'Peter', were riding horses. 'Peter' was the gem of them all – a Russian pony – 'Peter the Great' was his full name – dappled white with great chestnut patches. He took six of us children up and down hill to dancing classes at Mrs Graham's, Rednock, Dursley.

SHERBORNE GARDENERS

The carriage pair before 'Mother Bunch' and 'Charley' were 'Boffin' and 'Bella', and very smart and upstanding they looked when harnessed to the High Sheriffs carriage – a striking looking conveyance with its hammer-cloth, its coat-of-arms and its little perch for two footmen behind. It was in 1877 that my father filled what I lately heard described as 'the honourable but much to be avoided office of High Sheriff'.

My father was a member of the Duke of Beaufort's and Lord Fitzhardinge's hunts. The last used to meet sometimes at the Ridge. My father once lost his monocle out hunting and it was found in a ploughed field two years later and returned to him quite undamaged. Our two elder brothers and sister also hunted, but we three had as a steed only Jenny the donkey.

To return to the house. Beyond the stable yard was another in which were the 'shops' of the estate carpenter and blacksmith, old 'Daddy' Poole and his son Edward. Daddy was a dear, who used to call us twins his 'little sweethearts'. We loved his shop with its tools and wood-shavings and pots of paints, but Edward's had even greater attractions, with the huge bellows and the forge and an anvil and flying sparks, besides watching him shoe the great feet of the cart-horses.

On the other side of the house, a wide path ran down to the gardens, through lawns and shrubbery, by an iron bridge over a sunk road and across a stream to the greenhouses and kitchen garden. We loved the cheerful burbling stream which came from a reservoir above and fell in quite a respectable waterfall into the fernery, past our mother's special garden and the orchard, and flowed through the Valley of Butterflies and below the 'Dingle' into Waterley Bottom. The greenhouses were five in number and adjoining the 'stove' at one end of them was the cottage of William Workman, the head gardener, a great friend. We thought his cottage fascinating, as its top door opened from the kitchen garden, but downstairs was another door opening at a lower level into the orchard. Two little nieces lived with him and his wife, and I remember when one of them died being moved to tears when we sang with Mother at the drawing-room piano, 'Tender Shepherd, Thou hast stilled now Thy little lamb's brief weeping'.

Below the orchard were the shooting dogs' kennels. I remember 'Fidget', a little roan spaniel, and 'Beau' and 'Belle', retrievers, the companions of Henry Workman, the keeper. Workman was the name of many families round, and of our six gardeners three bore it – William, old Joe who lived in the Dingle

A RIDE ON THE ESTATE

cottage, and Albert at the Bowcote Lodge. He married our head laundry maid, Charlotte, and great was our excitement when their son Freddie arrived.

Bowcote Farm was the Home Farm then, and many happy times we had there. Single Gloucester cheeses were made, as well as butter, and I remember our kind Mistress of the Dairy who used to make tiny loaves for us and minute pats of butter like roses to eat with them. We knew all the cart-horses well: 'Prince' and 'Captain', 'Violet' and 'Blackbird', 'Polly' and 'Jerry'. These last were the special charges of David Poole, one of the carters, who lived in the lodge towards the Ridings. The cowman, Ephraim Woodward, lived in the 'Round House' on the road to Dursley. George Baglin looked after the pigs, and greatly did we enjoy watching him ladle out the swill for them in a bowl with a very long handle from two deep pits in one of the buildings.

The Bailiff, James Hancock, lived in the cottage at the far end of the plantations near the Dursley road. In the main lodge was Charles Hand, who worked in both stables and garden, and there was a Jim Baglin who cleaned the knives and shoes. We used to pick up sticks for his old mother, Biddy.

But the chief occasion for the picking up by us of sticks was the great bonfire on Guy Fawkes Day. We used to have one in the park – so large it could be seen from across the Severn, as we could see those over there. The maids in the workroom (where all the sewing for the house was done) used to make a huge Guy, and it was terrifying to see him being carried downstairs – a great, tall, white stuffed figure, always with a full matchbox in his pocket; there was great excitement when it caught fire and went off with a bang, and when the poor Guy himself fell down into the flames. There were fireworks afterwards and the roasting of potatoes in the embers.

We did not at all agree with our German governess, Fräulein Emmerich, who thought the bonfires were a great waste of wood! Fräulein found us, no doubt, very trying at times. I remember her once waving a copy-book to and fro, saying 'I should like to put this about your ears, right and left! right and left!' Her very nervous temperament was badly shaken one day when she was giving my eldest sister a music lesson, her little dog 'Bobbie' suddenly barked from underneath the chair on

2ND VBGR AT CAMP

which she was sitting. 'What has this confounded little cur altogether to seek here?' was Fräulein's passionate enquiry.

Of pets we had not many. I only remember one dog who lived in the house – a very dear rough-haired brown terrier mentioned above. One day my father brought back in the dogcart a real live goat from one of the tenants in the Vale. He used to come with us on walks like a dog.

On Sundays twelve of us and some other twelve servants went to the little church, three-quarters of a mile from the house. It was built by our great-uncle, and most picturesquely situated on a high wooded promontory, sloping steeply down into Waterley Bottom. The little church used to be pretty well filled, what with local farmers, the men who worked for us, and ourselves. I remember one Sunday afternoon a man came into church in the middle of a service to say a rick was on fire at Bowcote. The male part of the congregation left, as one man, and the clergyman came to my eldest sister and asked if he should preach the sermon. We did without a sermon that afternoon! In our young days the church bell was sometimes put to a more secular use than calling to worship. As when Mrs Park's bees were about to swarm, she was wont to ring it to summon her husband from the Ridge garden to wrestle with them.

Besides being Deputy Lieutenant and magistrate, my father was a captain in the 2nd Volunteer Battalion Gloucestershire Regiment, and one of the Yeomanry, the Royal Gloucestershire Hussars. We have a photograph of him in the uniform of the latter – very striking with its high spurred boots, sword, sabre-tache and busby, and the picturesque much-braided Hussars swing-jacket. My eldest brother was also a JP, and a lieutenant in the Volunteers. His coming-of-age was celebrated by the Volunteers doing manoeuvres in the park and by a fancy ball.

For the manoeuvres there was a plan marked out with little red flags, and this brings me to a very important member of our household, Jane Dominy, to all of us just 'Niny'. When my mother married she came to her as her maid, and when we left The Ridge I was the last of the family she lived with. She died a short time after I went to India as a missionary in 1914. Niny was always famous for the way she would keep things in case they might come in useful. Twenty-six years after the Volunteers'

LECHLADE

manoeuvres on my brother's coming-of-age I had a small nephew staying and had made a nine-hole golf-course in our little fields and, consulting Niny about flags for the greens, she produced the ones that had been used that day!

As regards young companions there were not many of our age in the neighbourhood. Besides the Grahams at Red nock, I can only remember the Revd C. Murray-Browne's at Stouts Hill, and further away, the Ricardos at Gatcombe, Minchinhampton.

At Kingscote in those days were Sir Nigel Kingscote, my mother's first cousin, and Lady Emily, his wife, a son and two daughters. My only remembrance of cousin Nigel Kingscote is of him at a dance at The Ridge trying in vain to persuade my small self-conscious self to let him pull me through the Lancers! Lady Emily, my godmother, was lady-in-waiting to Queen Alexandra when she was Princess of Wales, and woman of the bedchamher after she became queen. And so ends this record of a happy childhood. We left The Ridge in 1884 for Dorsetshire.

Miss E. M. Bengough

THE ROAD-MENDER

The road-mender lives in the little old original cottage at the corner of the lane as you turn to go up to Nightingale Farm, beyond the Roman ruins. The tenement is his own, and was his father's before him. It was really a kind of squatter's cottage. Someone or other, not very ambitious, came along, admired the spot, obtained material, built his house, and settled in it, there and then.

The little cottage is of one storey, and contains three fair-sized rooms – one for living, and two for sleeping. There is a fireplace at each extremity. The pantry is a small lean-to at one end, without the house. The original front was of rubble, but it has been modernized; brick has been substituted. A short while ago a pan of the front was nearly falling down, but after the old man got the old-age pension, he was able to get a few bricks and have the repairs executed. 'Times be lookin' up, a know,' the road-mender said; 'must do summat to 't now.' The back wall of the house is built close against the bank, that

PUESDOWN INN, NORTHLEACH.
Near the highest point
on the Cotswolds

THE PUESDOWN INN

is almost level with the eaves. Large elm-trees grow in the hedge there, and wave their tops high up. There, in the season, sing the thrush, the blackbird, the linnet, and the cuckoo. When the tempest howls through the elms and shakes the top of more pretentious dwellings and mansions, it leaves the little cottage unmoved; it is too humble for envy, even for that of the winds; they rage and fly along high above it. A small strip of garden is attached, protected by a box hedge, and running down the lane. The line of elms continues down the bank.

His father lived here before him. He worked on the highways too. When the old people died, the son took up his residence under the paternal roof, and here his family of four – two boys and two girls – were born. These are all grown up, and scattered to the four winds almost, and one is dead. He committed suicide. Entering the army, he served through the South African War in the cavalry; but as is so often the case, he contracted habits of dissoluteness, from which he could never free himself afterwards. At last, out of work, disheartened and penniless, baffled by fate and fortune, and overtaken at length by that worst of all weaknesses, he gave way to the impulse of self-destruction, and so ended his life. Happening to be near the railway one afternoon, and seeing an express coming towards

TOADSMOOR

him, he ran down the steep bank, clapped his hands together as a swimmer would do in taking the water, and dived straight under the wheels of the engine. The old man, living alone—his wife had been many years dead—was stunned with the news, and overwhelmed with sorrow. The old villagers shook their heads. 'Ah! he come to a bad end. Know'd a ood. That sowjerin done summat for ee.' His name is there, carved on the bark of the beeches that stand by the pool.

The old road-mender is nearly eighty now. He is very small in stature, but just over four feet high. His features are small and regular; he is fine looking—well-shaped nose, taper forehead, blue eyes, grey hair, moustache, and side-whiskers. His shoulders are bent a little—they have borne many a heavy sack of corn from the thresher to the granary—and he is half a cripple. His left leg is in the shape of a bow; in walking he swings this round somewhat, and especially if he has imbibed a glass or two of fourpenny; then he will have great difficulty in maintaining a dignified gait as he totters off, stick in hand, and basket on arm, down the road to his cottage. The old man is his own master, servant, and everything combined. He lights his fires, prepares his food, washes up and cleans the house, makes his own bed—is cook, chambermaid, and scullery-maid together. Often in the summer months he rises at four, and lights the fire to cook the sweet green peas and young 'taters'. After that he potters about till seven or eight, then goes to view his vegetable crops in the allotment; he has acquired great local fame as a horticulturist, and he usually tops the list for fine produce in the garden. After due inspection of the onion bed and potato patch, and comparing them with others in the field, he may visit the inn for a morning glass and a chat with the landlord; then, if it is fine, he lies down in the shade of the withy-tree, or elder boughs, till dinner-time, and very often all day, then loads himself with produce, and goes home to his cottage again. Here he cooks for tea or supper, eats the meal in silence, and retires about eight. The great problems of the day and hour do not disturb his manner of living; in spite of his losses and misfortunes he is happy and satisfied.

Alfred Williams

LARCHES AND WILD STRAWBERRIES

Near where a roadway to the right went to a cottage situated in the wood, and there was some amount of open ground, a portion was surrounded by wire-netting that left a space for the passage of the track in recognition of its being a public way. Within the netting were hen-coops dedicated to the use of pheasant-rearing, and a number of chicks, as yet quite young and with the appearance of quail, were running in the grass or answering to the cluck of their foster-mother hens.

The keeper was near at hand to object to anyone leaving the track-way, were it but to examine the specimens of 'vermin' that were hanging to the wire-netting that separated the woodland from the path. Gibbeted there were hawks of both the common species that had met their death from the gun whilst hovering suspiciously in the neighbourhood; also a crow or two, a magpie, a jay and a weasel. All of these had paid the penalty of their character, which, though natural, is but too well known to be inimical to the welfare of young pheasants.

A little further on and upward the rude track-way changed to a made road of whitish-yellow colour, some six feet broad. Beside it, on all sides, grew the species of willow-herb commonly called 'rose-bay'; its magenta petals and ruddy flower stalks producing the colour in this woodland which is so noticeable towards sunset when viewed from the distant ground of opposite hills. In places the red was intermingled with the violet of cranesbill, giving the roadside and the more open ground between the trees a fine appearance. On the right there was a thick wood composed of tall and straight-grown larches, and wood-pigeons were cooing there, the scolding tones of one father pigeon being prominent amongst the rest. A little girl was gathering wild strawberries in an open part of the wood. Near the road in this locality the ground was partly covered with a wild tangle of brambles, briars and furze. To the left there

BLOCKLEY

was a pretty view down to Winchcombe and beyond, over a fallow of finely-coloured clean earth, the bright red-brown being strewn with buff stones, and on the ground adjacent were green crops, a patch of charlock of brilliant yellow, the crimson of sainfoin and the purple of clover, the neutral drab of the hay in cocks that was being carted, the blue-green distances of hill and vale, and the quiet blue and white of the July sky.

John Henry Garrett

LIFE IN THE WORKHOUSE

CIRENCESTER UNION

We found ourselves at the gate at half-past ten in the morning, and while waiting for admission noticed the printed order that the inmates are allowed to see their friends on Mondays and Fridays, from one o'clock till four, and on no other occasions, except under special circumstances.

As the district is purely agricultural, the inmates are chiefly of that class. The average wage of the day labourer is nine shillings a week; and as it is a matter of impossibility that the man and wife can bring up a family and save out of this for old age, even if they do get a nice little cottage and bit of garden for five pounds a year, it is but natural that they should end their days here, when work fails them through old age or sickness.

There were many more old men than women in the house the day we were there; and we heard from the matron that the old women can postpone their coming in for weeks or even months by the variety of work they can put their hands to – whereas the men can do but one kind of work, and when that fails all is over with them. Those not agricultural labourers, who find themselves paupers, have as a rule arrived at this condition through drink.

DURSLEY UNION WORKHOUSE

The children here, as at other workhouses, are almost all illegitimate. The orphans, twelve at present, are boarded out in the villages round about. A lady visitor is supposed to pay constant visits to the several homes, and keep a supervision over them in order that the little ones may be well treated.

One of the great obstacles to a child's well-being in a workhouse is that just as the matron and teacher are beginning to see a decided improvement in a girl or boy, the mother may come and take them away, and, after exposing them to every kind of foul living, bring them back again. It makes the reclaiming and teaching them well-nigh hopeless.

We found everything spotlessly clean but very bare. Take the boys' day-room for example, which had stone floors, bare walls and two forms for furniture; their play-yard outside being equally bare; there was an absence of pictures and games, or of anything that would afford the slightest amusement.

We were exceedingly pleased with the school-room, its thirty scholars and gentle little school-mistress, the daughter of the master and matron. The children looked happy and industrious; their sewing, writing, and spelling were good. The chaplain who lives in the town comes once a month to give religious instruction.

As a rule, the children are docile and easily managed.

For the infirmary there is a trained nurse under the authority of the matron; she has a sitting-room and bedroom, and a bell communicating with her apartments hangs in each sick ward.

Infectious diseases are not admitted, but are taken to a building a mile off, provided and governed by the sanitary authorities.

The chronic sick ward was the brightest we had seen, with its yellow quilts, gay pictures, books and flowers.

There should be, I think, a comb and brush for each bed: as it is, there are four or five brushes, and but one comb for each ward!

In the nursery were four babies. One pretty little mite of two years old was fast pining away, and her mother, who was only twenty-one, and of course single, had two other children in the house! We saw

CASTLE STREET, CIRENCESTER

her helping in the kitchen with apparently no shame at her position.

One dormitory is devoted to mothers with babies, who are allowed to keep them at night until they are two years old.

The old people breakfast on porridge and bread, while the infirm, the laundry women and the wards-women have bread, butter, tea, milk and sugar and at night, all except the children have tea.

In the kitchen the inevitable pea-soup was being prepared for dinner for all the inmates, except the children, who were going to have rice and milk. A pound and a half of meat goes to the gallon of water; but it so happens that now and then they boil a large quantity of beef, and then the liquor is used instead of water, and with the addition of vegetables an exceedingly good soup is made.

The dining hall is of fair size, and here all take food together in the presence of a superintendent; and here on Sundays the chaplain holds service.

I think the food is very good and varied and well cooked. Two days in the week they have boiled bacon and two vegetables, two days meat and two vegetables, two days pea-soup, and another day beef and potatoes. The average cost per head for maintenance and clothing is 3s. 8½d. a week.

They deal with casuals on the Berkshire system, which is that the tramp obtains from the police a pass with his name and age written on it together with his destination. This he takes to the union, and on his leaving the master fills in the name of the next union on the direct route to his destination, and also the places on the road where he may get bread. So, if a man comes with a brand-new ticket, or one showing he is out of his proper route, he is deprived of his liberty for a day and made to work, as he is considered a loafer. Of course the men do what they can to circumvent this, tearing up their tickets whenever they get a chance, and sometimes the lane outside is strewn with torn-up tickets.

The employment given is stone-breaking, oakum picking, and gardening.

The casuals are lodged in cells, each of which has a bell, and on its being rung a red indicator outside the door falls down, and is at once clearly seen by the person in charge.

CLAPHAM, GLOUCESTER

GLOUCESTER UNION

Our next visit was to the Gloucester Workhouse, which is a contrast to Cirencester in that it stands practically on the railway, just outside the station.

Ten years ago this workhouse was so filthy and neglected that, we are assured, it would have been impossible for us to have gone through it, and now, notwithstanding its proximity to the railway, everything in it and about it is scrupulously clean and orderly.

Among the inmates there are many old agricultural labourers, and a large number of factory women, dock labourers and wagon hands, beside many deserted women and women with families – drink being in a great measure the cause of the latter classes finding themselves here.

Beside the master and matron, the paid officers consist of the schoolmaster and mistress, an industrial trainer, a nurse, porter, cook, tramp-master and mistress, a tailor and shoemaker. The two last teach their trades to the boys, who not infrequently develop into very good shoemakers, tailors, and gardeners, trades which serve them in good stead both here and in the Colonies, whither many of the boys go after leaving the house.

The children are kept until they are twelve or fourteen, and have passed the fourth standard, which, being the minimum necessary for the wage-earning community, means reading with intelligence, writing clearly and correctly from dictation, and working sums rapidly in the compound rules of arithmetic.

One of the great wants in the workhouse for the girls who have to go out to service has been the industrial training necessary for a small household. Everything is on so large a scale that when they first go out to service they are confused at finding themselves in a small kitchen; for example, they cannot light an ordinary fire, they know nothing of the use of the saucepan or gridiron, they are unable from sheer ignorance of their surroundings to perform the duties of their new position, and they lose heart and often head too, and turn out a failure.

BATSFORD

The food is good and varied; instead of porridge, the adults have tea and bread and butter, while the children have bread and milk.

The wardswomen and washers are allowed half a pint of beer a day, and the old men over sixty an ounce of tobacco a week.

The infirmary is exceedingly well cared for, the wards are bright, and there is a nice little hospital kitchen, where beef tea or any little extra is prepared.

The casual wards are on the cell system.

The death rate is very low.

Altogether this workhouse is a credit to the master and matron as well as to the guardians.

Mrs Brewer, Sunday at Home

GOODBYE POOR BUNNY

This afternoon I visited Cocklebury Farm and Cottage. Patience Ferris told me a strange story. A fortnight ago her boy Jacob, who works for Farmer Matthews at Cocklebury, was wandering about upon the Mount (overlooking the deep railway cutting) eating his dinner. He saw on the opposite railway bank a man and boy carrying a spade and a long box. The man put down the box on the bank and began to dig. Then he saw Jacob Ferris watching him and left off digging and walked away. Jacob hid himself behind a tree and presently the man, thinking himself unobserved, came back and went on with his digging. Jacob saw him dig a hole in the railway bank and then he and the boy laid the long box in the hole, filled it up, and went away. At night Jacob said to the other farm lad, Robert Matthews, 'Let us go and dig that box up, there's money in it and we'll go halves.' The two boys went in the dark, found the place, and dug up the box. It was fastened tight, the lid being screwed down with three screws like a coffin. The boys opened the box and found inside it something soft pinned

PAINSWICK

up in paper which smelt very bad. They did not open the parcel but left the box and its contents under the hedge of the 'Barn Ground' behind Rawlings Farmhouse, and Jacob came home and told his parents what he had seen. Patience thought the matter should be looked into and asked William her husband to go and examine the box, but if he found anything was wrong not to bring it to their cottage. William went and found the box as the boys has said under the hedge and took it to the farm to examine it. From what he saw he thought it right to send for a policeman to examine and open the parcel. But that night the Union was on fire and the policeman was not at the station. Before the policeman could be found Ralph Knight had come up to Rawlings by accident. He looked at the mysterious box and noticed on the lid some writing, which had unfortunately escaped William's notice. The writing on the box was this, 'Goodbye, poor Bunny. 1876'. When the parcel was opened it was found to contain the body of a rabbit skinned. It was a pet rabbit belonging to the boy whom Jacob Ferris had seen with the man (who was the boy's father) burying the suspicions-looking box. The affair found its way into the county papers and for a week town and country have been in an uproar of laughter and delight. Now whenever Jacob Ferris and the policeman appear they are saluted by ironical cries of 'Goodbye, poor Bunny. 1876'.

POVERTY AND HUNGER

Went to see old Caroline Farmer and read to her the latter part of Luke vii. On my way thither I fell in with a boy in the lane named George Wells. He was going to beg a bit of bread from a woman who lived at the corner of the Common under the Three Firs. He said he did not know the name of the woman but she knew his mother and often gave him a bit of bread when he was hungry. His mother was a cripple and had no parish relief, sold cabbage nets and had nothing to give him for dinner. The boy's face looked pale, pinched and hungry.

CHIPPING CAMPDEN HOUSE

A BARBAROUS CLERGYMAN

We are in trouble at the school now because a few days ago Mr Ashe came angrily in to Miss Bland the schoolmistress and ordered her always to keep all three windows and the door of the schoolroom open during schooltime, except in very cold weather when one window might be shut. He said in a fierce determined way, 'This is my school and I will have my word attended to. If you don't do as I tell you, Miss Bland, instead of being your friend I'll be your enemy.' What a speech for an elderly clergyman. It is almost incredible. And there are the poor little children crying with the cold. Cruel. Barbarous. And of course the parents are indignant and the numbers of the children falling off.

Francis Kilvert

THE BASHFUL FATHER

When a birth takes place in a village, news of it is quickly passed from house to house; everyone in the parish is soon made aware of the circumstance; it is quite a public event. 'What is it; a bwoy or a girrul?' is the first question asked; and afterwards, 'Wha's ee's name gwain to be?' In due time the infant is baptized, often in the middle of a service. If it is a first born, and the rustic husband is prevailed upon to attend, he will be extremely bashful and awkward, blushing like a schoolgirl. If the father works on the farm, his mates will expect to be treated to a glass or two of ale, to 'wet the youngster', and 'drenk 'is 'ealth', and the wish is acceded to good-humouredly.

Alfred Williams

THE PASSING OF THE GOOD SQUIRE

My father had decided, after the founding of the church in his own home, to observe the day of consecration annually by asking the whole parish to dinner. Huge tents were fashioned out of rick-cloths,

JOHN AND MARY HALL, BLEDINGTON

for it was many years before the invention of the modern marquee. Several rows of tables extended from end to end; the tenant farmers acted as carvers; their wives, daughters, and others, as waiters; and every man, woman, and child in the parish sat down to roast beef and mutton and plum-pudding, to be washed down with beer or cider, as the diner wished.

In the early days, and for many years, all the old men, and also the majority of the middle-aged, invariably attended in smock-frocks, many of these garments being beautiful examples of their wives' needlework; the older women appearing in the red shawl, then the full dress in rural England for all great functions.

The annual dinner, on a day in the early spring, became in time a very marked occasion in the parish. Dates were reckoned by it, and the ages of most of the children were computed by the number of dinners that had elapsed from date of birth; it was always: 'Jane, or our William, will be seven come dinner'; or "T'will be twenty years last dinner since my good man was took.' The dinner was thus the landmark for all when a survey was taken of the passing years.

But as time went on it was also something else. To look back at a long succession of these great feasts is to see now how accurately they reflected the change that must ever wait upon the passing of time. It was a happy, homely gathering, as of one great family party, where all were known to one another, and where each loved the squire dearly, as the truest friend they could turn to when any ill befell them or theirs. The dinner ended, either the vicar or a principal tenant proposed the squire's health, who, in his reply, marked always by no little wit, but always also by a serious sentence or two, never failed to refer to the place as 'a happy and united parish'.

Of the truth of this there was no room for doubt. There was friendliness on all hands, and not on this parish festival alone, but equally at the door of every cottage and farm on any day throughout the year; with an honest smile, and an invitation to 'come in and make yourself at home', in old-fashioned, English welcome. In the afternoon there were cricket and football and other games: all the grounds were thrown open; the tenant farmers and their families came to tea; and when the beauties of the spring day

BATSFORD

waned, the great bell in the church tower was set swinging, and shortly afterwards the whole parish trooped across the park for the evening service that closed the memorable day.

It has all long since gone, though it is not even now entirely forgotten. It took a long time going, for these anniversary dinners were held annually for nearly forty years, till finally they might almost have been said to have brought about their own end. There was no perceptible lack of warmth in the friendship evinced, and there was very certainly no falling-off in the love that was shown for the squire, and that took the form as he grew old of something approaching reverence. It was still a happy gathering, and the parish was a united one to the very last dinner, and beyond it. But, at the same time, the smock-frocks grew fewer in numbers, till one or two alone remained, and the red shawls altogether disappeared.

The atmosphere was slowly changing. The aristocratic look of the old men and the perfect manner of the older women were giving place to something different, and certainly less pleasing. Deference and respect for the aged was dying out with the young, and the friendliness of the old generation was being slowly eclipsed by the civility of the new. Broadcloth slowly replaced old-fashioned corduroy and fustian; the simplicity of the older women's

FAIRFORD

THE CHEDWORTH BAND

COURT FARM, CHIPPING CAMPDEN

dresses and bonnets and their treasured bits of needlework began to savour of a past age, being thrown into the shade by the colours, the flowers and feathers of their daughters and of the younger married folk. Even the children were not left in many cases without their bit of finery. At the same time, and year by year, a growing awkwardness and shyness of manner took the place of former ready geniality; the homeliness of the whole gathering in large part gradually disappeared, and by degrees many of those who had been eager and content to dine, were now all too ready to wait at table while their fathers and their mothers ate.

No one knew it was the last dinner. The squire was growing old, though outwardly retaining all his vigour and alertness of mind. It was with difficulty that he was persuaded not to refer to its being the last dinner in his usual speech. He knew that his days were numbered. He walked slowly over to the tents and said a few sentences, marked by all his keen sense of fun, no less than by that seriousness that lay always at the back of him; and though he made no reference to the termination of a festival, many present realised to the full that 'Dinner' had come to an end with his closing words.

He never abated one jot of his industry; he never spared himself in any way. He went straight on as though he had not been warned that the end might come at any instant. He no longer rode, but drove to Gloucester in a small open pony-trap; and when he returned at night, again and again wet through, he treated it all as a joke, and was in no hurry whatever to change his clothes.

It came at last. The squire was going.

He had had a hard day's work at home, and when the afternoon closed in he left the house and walked a little way across the park, a collie that either occupied the one armchair in his room, or lay outside his door, accompanying him.

The men told afterwards that, on their way home from work, they had seen him walking slowly through the orchards. He, too, was going home. That evening their squire lay dead – dying as he would have wished to die; and when morning dawned the great bell, with muffled tongue, told many far and wide that the best friend they ever had was gone.

There is little need to say more; but on the golden autumn day when he was laid to rest, the poor, especially, flocked from town and parish, and all the country round, to pay their tribute; and many, young and old, men and women, were seen to be in tears.

The 'Good Squire' was dead.

Major Gambier-Parry

THE CHEDWORTH BAND

The Cotswold folk on the whole are fond of music, though they have not a large amount of talent for it. The Chedworth band still goes the round of villages once or twice a year. These men are the descendants of the 'old village musicians', who, to quote from the Strand Musical Magazine for September 1897, 'led the Psalmody in the village church sixty years ago with stringed and wind instruments. Mr Charles Smith, of Chedworth, remembers playing the clarionet in Handel's Zadok the Priest, performed there in 1838 in honour of the Queen's accession.' He talks of a band of twelve, made up of strings and wood-wind.

I am bound to say that the music produced by the Chedworth band at the present day, though decidedly creditable in such an old-world village, is rather like the Roman remains for which the district is so famous; it savours somewhat of the prehistoric. But when the band comes round and plays in the hall of my house on Christmas Eve, I have many a pleasant chat with the Chedworth musicians; they are so delightfully enthusiastic, and so grateful for being allowed to play. When I gave them a cup of tea they kept repeating, 'A thousand thanks for all your kindness, sir.'

THE HAWKER

A strange-looking traveller, with slouching gait and mouldy wide-awake hat, passes through the hamlet occasionally, leading a donkey in a cart. This is one of the old-fashioned hawkers. These men are usually poachers or receivers of poached goods. They are not averse to paying a small sum for a basket of trout or a few partridges, pheasants, hares or rabbits in the game season; whilst in spring they deal in a small way in the eggs of game birds. Often as not this class of man is accompanied by a couple of dogs, marvellously trained in the art of hunting the coverts and 'retrieving' a pheasant or a rabbit which may be crouching in the underwood. Hares, too, are taken by dogs in the open fields. One never finds out much about these gentry from the natives. Even the keeper is reticent on the subject. 'A sart of a harf-witted fellow' is Tom Peregrine's description of this very suspicious-looking traveller.

The better sort of carrier, who calls daily at the great house with all kinds of goods and parcels from the big town seven miles off, is occasionally not averse to a little poaching in the roadside fields among the hares. The carriers are a great feature of these rural villages; they are generally good fellows, though some of them are a bit too fond of the bottle on Saturday nights.

J. Arthur Gibbs

FARMER TULL

Farmer Tull was one of the very old school, who had done fairly well in his time, but had not the faculty of making the most of his earnings. Moreover he was altogether too easy going and too generous to make a pile on his small farm. He lived well, paid high wages, cared for no man, and was fond – perhaps over-fond – of little drops of gin; he would have done better if he had lived more frugally, but he was not going to starve himself, not he! and he had no relatives to leave anything to. In the end he had to partake of charity himself.

''Tis main dull yer this marnin', chaps. Bistn't agwain to seng us a bit of a song to liven us up narn a bit, Jimmy?' the old man said one day in the hayfield. So Jimmy, the boy, struck up with lines from an old agricultural song, used in the times of the riots, and handed down to that generation:

O you working men of England,
Take heed to what I say,
And have no rest, but do your best
To get a fair day's pay.

'Yer, that 'ull do, that 'ull do. Dwun want to yer no more o' that. Casn't thenk o' nothin' else no different to that?' Jimmy thought a minute, then broke out again:

O you big-bellied farmers, you pot-bellied farmers,
Your pride and ambition shall soon be brought low.

'Damn tha, shet up! Tha's ten times wuss than ever. Begad, if I yers any more o' that I'll fetch tha one wi' my crab. Gee up, Tom, and le's get out o' the rawd an' 'em. Zend the jar in and ha'n villed when a's empty, and dwun go adry. You wimmin come in to the varm a' dinner-time, missus 'ull gi' ee zummat to aat.' The springs of the cart went down bump! at crossing the trenches, and nearly pitched the old fellow out on his head when they rose again; he made his way across the field and round into the yard. There was a little stone platform with several steps, which reached level with the shafts of the cart; here

TEWKESBURY

he mounted and dismounted from the vehicle, assisted by his wife and one of the workmen; it was quite a ceremony, and lasted nearly ten minutes.

Alfred Williams

THE ROWING TOUR

We arrived at Tewkesbury at 6 p.m. Our route then lay down the Severn, and we had to pass through a lock from one river to the other. We went underneath a very queer old stone bridge, and passed a number of wharves and factories. When we got to the lock, we found some lighters going through, and as we did not care about waiting, we turned back and landed at the Boathouse, where we left the boat for the night with instructions for it to be ready for us by nine o'clock the next morning. We were recommended to go to the Swan Hotel, as being the best in the place, and we accordingly walked along the principal street for a considerable distance, until we reached it. Our impression of the town was anything but lively. The shops were all closed, as if it were Sunday, and those few people that were about, stared at us as if we had been wild beasts. On arriving at the hotel we ordered supper, changed our things, wrote some letters and then went out for a stroll and to see the Abbey, the only place of interest in the town, I believe, and this did not prove particularly interesting to us, as it was locked up for the day, and the outside was certainly not beautiful. We were much struck with the melancholy appearance of the town; on enquiry we heard that nearly all the shops shut at 5 p.m. on Thursday, so we were unfortunate in our day.

It is altogether a very queer old place, and looked as if it had been built in the year 1: the houses are very antedeluvian and irregular, hardly two alike, and the shops (at least those that were open) were very small and insignificant. One, I noticed, was marked over the door 'Fruiterer' and inside the place was full of old clothes, and at a toy-shop tea and coffee were dispensed behind the counter. We had supper at 8, and were much amused at the waitress, who, after we had sent her for something, begged us to make up our minds all at once what we wanted, and she would fetch the lot altogether, as she

A BAPTISM AT CRICKLADE

didn't like running up and down stairs so often. We replied that we could not measure off our appetites to a crumb, and of course as we finished the chops, the milk, and the butter etc. at different times, and almost invariably required a fresh supply, it was hardly to be expected we could comply with her polite request. After tea we sat out on the balcony and smoked, and watched the volatilities of some young dressmakers through an open window in the opposite house. When it was dark, we took a walk into the country at the back of the town, and returned to bed at 10.

Memo: When you go to Tewkesbury, don't stop at the Swan Hotel, the place is dirty, the attendance is inefficient and the charges are very stiff.

Howard Williams

THE BAPTISM

There was a great splash, and a tall young woman was perceived to be in the baptismal pool, her arms waving above her head, and her figure held upright in the water by the inflation of the air underneath her crinoline which was blown out like a bladder, as in some extravagant old fashion-plate. Whether her feet touched the bottom I cannot say, but I suppose they did so. An indescribable turmoil of shrieks and cries followed on this extraordinary apparition. A great many people excitedly called upon other people to be calm and an instance was given of the remark of James Smith that

He who, in quest of quiet, 'Silence!' hoots
Is apt to make the hubbub he imputes.

The young woman, in a more or less fainting condition, was presently removed from the water, and taken into the sort of tent which was prepared for candidates. It was found that she herself had wished

BIBURY

to be a candidate and had earnestly desired to be baptized, but this had been forbidden by her parents. On the supposition that she fell in by accident, a pious coincidence was detected in this affair; the Lord had pre-ordained that she should be baptized in spite of all opposition. But my father, in his shrewd way, doubted. He pointed out to us, next morning, that, in the first place, she had not, in any sense, been baptized, as her head had not been immersed; and that, in the second place, she must have deliberately jumped in, since, had she stumbled and fallen forward, her hands and face would have struck the water, whereas they remained quite dry. She belonged, however, to the neighbour congregation, and we had no responsibility to pursue the enquiry any further.

Edmund Goose

SHORTWOOD CHAPEL

. . . And then the baptisms. What times of refreshing they were! All these things come to my mind. As one stands here, one cannot but think one's life is more of the past than of the present.

I cannot but remember the many times I have preached here myself. A good many times our dear pastor, Mr Newman, called upon me to speak to the congregation here. We Dissenters have often been told we are political, that we care very much more for our church and denomination than we do for the Gospel. We are often told that our preaching of the Gospel is only a secondary matter, that we are very sectarian; and, indeed, the Baptists are supposed to be the narrowest of men, who have very little thought but of dipping people and getting them to be called Baptists. I lived among you many years, and knew what passed, and I can most emphatically say it was not so here. I never heard a political, or denominational, or sectarian sermon.

Dr Underhill

MISERDEN

STRONG BEER AND SIMS

The ancient inn, with its spreading walnut tree and sturdy, iron-bound stocks nearby, was famed for its generous home-brewed beer. Once I had tasted it and admired its choice flavour, I wanted to know how to make it. To this end I spent an evening with the landlord and he taught me the secret and the whole formula of the trade.

'Many people,' said he, 'use but three things in brewing – malt, hops and water – and of them make three kinds of liquor: strong beer, fresh beer and sims.'

'Strong beer I know, and fresh beer I know, but sims I do not know. What is sims?' I queried.

'It sims like beer, but it isn't,' answered he.

'Then,' said I, quoting an old rhyme that I once heard at harvest-home,

"This puts me in mind of Dame Trot
when she began to brew:
She took half-a-peck of stale malt and half-a-peck of
new;
She made forty gallons of black strap,
And forty gallons of wivvy wink,
And forty gallons of terrible drink."
And this must be some of the terrible drink.'

'Brewing is like a fat pig; it's all profit. You can sell

COMPTON ABDALE

CHARLES ANDREWS, WILLERSEY

everything, even to the skimmings,' proceeded the landlord.

'Teach me how to make it,' I replied.

'A bushel of malt and one pound of hops will make eighteen gallons of beer and nine gallons of ale; but if you want body in it just do as I tell you. Boil your water for the mash and empty it into the tub, steeping the hops in a separate vessel. When the steam has gone off the tub, so that you can see your face in the water, and not before, put in your malt and stir it, then cover with a sack and leave it for nine hours, giving it a rout now and then. In the meantime, clean out your casks and have your cooling tub ready. Draw off the sweet-wort, set the grains aside for the ale, put the liquor, with the hops, into the boiler, which must be iron or copper, and not zinc, and simmer for one hour. And now, if you want extra good beer, taps on old sycamore tree with an augur and get a quart of juice and mix it with the liquor; or get a bunch of carrots, parsnips, or beetroot, split them with a knife, and throw them into the boiler. At the end of an hour strain into the cooling vat, saving the hops, and mix a dozen pounds of coarse brown sugar, or treacle, with the sweet-wort and put in the barm at blood-heat. The following morning take what barm you require, put it into strong bottles and bury it in the earth, where it will keep as long as you please; and remember that barm wants changing for seed, and that a tablespoonful of barm with a little brandy is the best thing in the world for a stoppage and has saved many a man's life. If you wish you can put it on the cask the same night; but it will be better to wait for twenty-four hours at least. Well cork the barrel and fill to the bung hole, saving a little to make up for each day's waste. Look at the barrel to see that it ferments. At the end of a fortnight take two handfuls of dry hops and put them into the barrel, stir with a stick and bung up. To make new beer appear old pour a little vinegar into the bung hole; but to be good and strong it needs to be kept from six to twelve months; that is, from October till October comes again.'

Alfred Williams

CHALFORD HILL

SCIENTIFIC PIG-KEEPING

I met Willum at the usual place a few evenings ago.

'Good evening, Willum,' I said; and the glibness with which I brought out the old man's name reminded me of an incident which occurred in our village during the summer. Old Betty Turner had got her eldest daughter's son down from London, and being desirous of obtaining that Gloucestershire delicacy called 'chitlings' sent her precocious grandson to the bacon factory for some in the raw state. The boy was a typical Cockney. He asked the man at the factory for a 'bucket of inwards'. The slayer of pigs cast a look of disgust on the lad and it was not for some moments that he gathered what was wanted. But the bucket which the boy carried assisted his perceptions. 'Doost thee myen a bukkut o' innards?' he cried. The boy concluded that it was even so, but in telling me the incident he naively remarked, 'They do talk funny down hyar, don't they?'

In reply to my query as to his health Willum said, 'O! I be a' right, but not just as sprack as I shud like, these blamed east winds a' gid I the rumatiks.'

I suppose it must have been the recollection of the above incident, or it might have been the odour arising from Willum's boots; at any rate my thoughts turned to pigs. 'Everybody seems to keep a pig,' I remarked.

'Oi! Oi,' said Willum, 'but peg kipping yeny wot it usent to be. Now I a' kep a peg ever zence I woz married and I allus reckon to have a zide o' bacon to cut at. But Lard bless ye thur yent dree men in the villij as knaws 'ow to cure a bit o' bacon now, and zence old Dan'l Jones died I a' had a rare old job to cum across anybody as could even kill a peg.'

I said I had been told that it did not pay to keep pigs in these days.

The old man was quite vicious as he replied: 'Pay! A' coorse it dwunt pay. Thur's Nalus Pickwick kep a peg and got a book called – Lar' bless my zawl what was thuk thur book called – why "Zyentific Peg Kipping". Nalus used to cart that thuk book about wi' un and spend zumtimes as much as a zhillun in Stroud for zum zart o' stuff as the book zed ud make the pegs vat. Wun day he comes to I and zays, "Willum," he zays, "do 'e come and look at our peg." Well, I went and looked at un and I zed, zays

WRAGG CASTLE FARM, PITCHCOMBE

I, "Nalus thee'st better kill un or else her'll be a d'yed un." Nalus went off down the bottom to get a butcher, but avoor they cood get back the peg was d'yed. But they killed thuk ther peg all the zame and I dwunt thenk as Nalus lost more than half a zuvrin by un.'

I joined in Willum's laugh, but not very heartily, for I wondered how many pigs killed after they were dead I had partaken of

'You zee tis like this ere,' continued Willum, 'if you kips a peg zo as to ave plenty o' bacon to cut and kum agyen at, the peg pays. But nowadays evrybody zells thur pegs an' lets them as buys um make all the profit. Now thur was Jakob Tanner. Jakob used to kip his couple o' pegs and did vurry well oot on urn as long as the childurn woz yung and 'ad to yet wot woz put avoor um. But when Jakob an' his missis was left alone Jakob got the lumbago wun day and the missis had to tyuk the pegs thur vood. "Jakob," her zays, "if I a' got to veed the pegs I be agwoing to 'ave sum o' the profits." Zo now Jakob a' got to buy the missis a new hat or zummat when the pegs be zold. Natral enuf thur yent much profit left for Jakob now.'

I suggested that pigs were very dirty animals, and I wondered how we could so enjoy our bacon for breakfast.

'Now that's wur you do make a gurt mistake,' said Willum, 'Ther yent a cleaner animal than a peg when they be properly looked ater. I suppose I a' had to do wi' zum thousands on um in my time, and I never knawed wun as vouled his sleeping place, an' that's more than you can zay o' most animals. Why Lor' bless yer, zur, a peg is more like a human being than any other theng as lives. Old Doctor Vizzik as died last yur used to tell I as thur insides were nearer like ourn than any other animal. An' I a' noticed the look in thur eyes an' if you'll believe I thur wuz just the zame look in Ted Robert's eyes when the doctor told un he wuz a' gwoing to die as I 'av zid in the peg's eyes when the butcher was in the garden. An' when the zow a' had a litter o' yung uns why I 'av zid just the zame look in her eyes as my old 'ooman used to 'ave when our yung uns was barn. Bless 'e, zur, pegs and we be vurry much alike.'

We had reached Willum's cottage by this time, but the old man stood and talked.

'Talking o' pegs', he said, "minds I o' wot the missis was rading tuther night in the *Stroud News* about zum doctor or other as zed as 'ow we ought to tyuk a male o' sand zumtimes. When Nalus Pickwick,

FAIRFORD

as I was a' telling ye on just now, had got his fust peg and was a' trying to brang un up on "Zyentific Peg Kipping" the peg wun day 'oodn't stand up and his tail wuz as straight as thuk thur spout. Nalus dosed un up wi' wot the book zed, but the peg's tail 'oodn't curl no'ow. Zo Nalus kums down an' zays, "Willum, wot dust thenk I'd better gi'e the peg to make his tail curl?"

"Why," zays I, "thee go an' get half a bukkut o' small coal and let the peg yet it."

Nalus thought as how I wuz a joking at fust, but ater a bit he went an' got a han'ful o' small coal and looked over the sty and zed "Chuk, chuk." But the peg only grunted and 'oodn't get up, so Nalus goes inzide and put his hand to the peg's snout. Her vurry zoon skrunched up the small coal and looked for zum moor. Ater about the zixth 'andful her got up, and avoor night her tail was as curly as a corkscrew.'

With this little reminiscence Willum turned towards the door and I wished him good-night.

G. Edmund Hall

AN OVER-WORKED MOTHER

Lady Stradbroke, in *The Times* of December 1878, urging, necessarily enough, her fellow-women to give more help to their poorer sisters, says – 'Ready-made clothes are an immense boon to the poor; the overworked mother has hardly time to mend and darn, and bake, and wash, and nurse the baby, much less to make clothes for herself and husband and children.' I can give her an instance of this and more being done. 'The mother', who never thought about the word 'overworked', was a Gloucestershire woman, whose life was well known to my family and myself. She married at eighteen, her husband being about the same age. His wages as an agricultural labourer were never more than 15s. a week. She worked in the fields from eight to six, earning 10d. a day. She brought up nine children, made and mended all the clothes worn by them, her husband, and herself, until her sons and daughters were old

ARLINGTON ROW, BIBURY

enough to get their own. She was always up at five, washing-days at four. Went to bed between nine and ten. In harvest-time she would get the children up at two, be off with them to any field within walking distance, and begin gleaning as soon as it was light. On Saturdays her field-work was over at one, after which she would walk to the town, three miles, carrying often a basket of clothes for a neighbouring laundress, buy her 'marketing', as she called it, and carry home, with the rest of her little parcels, two pecks of flour. On Saturday evenings she baked, and would sometimes make a pair of trousers or a smock-frock, besides washing and ironing a few things that the children wanted for Sunday, and often working till midnight. She was a very regular attendant at the church services, which were a real pleasure to her. There were few gifts in her days; her only ones were, on the 30th of January in each year, a loaf of bread and material for one shirt. Her children began to work 'almost as soon as they could toddle', as one of them told me today. I may add that she was a strong, handsome, cheerful woman to the last, and lived to a good old age. Her children grew up respectable men and women, and her now numerous grandchildren are, without exception, the same, some of them in good positions, and all with a great capacity for work.

J.G. Gloucestershire Notes & Queries

GET THE ZAA BWOY

Many ridiculous things happen in the villages and are talked about and laughed at there, but are unknown to the outside world. There is the tale of a villager whose wife sent him to the little shop for needles, cotton, and thread. The old fellow, being unable to read, and of weak memory, was forced to repeat the names of the articles aloud upon the way to the shop. As he was passing down the hill repeating the words, 'Needles, cotton, thread. Needles, cotton, thread,' he stepped on a slide that the children had made in the road, slipped, and fell upon his back. In the confusion he forgot his needles, cotton, thread, and went on his way and burst into the shop, crying: 'Rasm, pitch, and tar! Rasm, pitch and tar!'

'Maester, maester,' cried the farm-boy one day, rushing into the kitchen in a state of great excitement, 'the caaf got 'is yed droo the gyet an' caan't get un out agyen!'

'Get the zaa, bwoy. Get the zaa, an' zas 'n out,' the farmer answered. Thereupon the boy got the saw and started to saw off the calf's head.

'Dang the bwoy! Why dissent zaa the gyet?' the farmer cried. Then, turning to his wife, he said: 'Never mind, missis, we shall hae plenty o' bif now.'

CARL THE CARTER

On coming up from Fairford to Northleach, I was saluted by no less than eighteen persons, chiefly carters and shepherds in company with their teams and flocks, either on the road or in the fields and farmyards adjoining she highway. This speaks for itself, and discovers the warm heartedness and sociability of the Cotswold peasant folk. Theirs is a lonely life, and doubtless they love to see a fresh face now and then, and take comfort in exchanging a few words with a sympathetic stranger.

As I was leaning on the wall, chatting with a carter who was at plough in the field, a middle-aged woman, bearing a basket of goods bought in the town, came up the hill and, after a respectful nod to me, addressed the carter in a shrill piping voice:

'Ev you a-yerd from Car-rl?'

'No,' replied he.

'We 'ev 'ed a letter,' she continued. ''E yent agwain on at all well. A no business to a left Calcutt. A was barn ther' an' brought up ther', an' a'd never bi away afoore till a tuk this fit in is 'ed. But a wunt stop away long. A'll break 'is 'eart if a do. Poor Car-rl! A cried all the way ther', an' a bin that miserable ever since a don' know what to do wi' 'itself. A'll never finish the twelve months out.'

'Poor Carl', as I learned, was a Cotswold carter who had been at one situation all his life and had only recently shifted to another village, with the result intimated in the good-wife's conversation.

The source of the Coln is near Charlton Abbots, about twelve miles to the north of Cirencester. From that point the river runs murmuring past the richly wooded slopes of Chedworth. Now it takes an easterly course, winding round through the old-fashioned villages of Coln St Denis, Coln Rogers, and Winson, and presently reaches the picturesque hamlet of Ablington, with its grand old manor house and the quiet beauty of its farms and cottages.

Bibury is the next village on the stream. Here the river is joined by a considerable spring that leaps out of the hillside, the waters of which scarcely vary, even after the driest summer. Near this is a commodious inn and a trout fishery, at which young fish for stocking the river are hatched and reared. Two large mills stand on the stream, and the ruins of a woollen factory are visible in a meadow not far from the banks.

The upper mill is silent now, but the one lower down, at Bibury, is still active and does a moderate amount of work, though only grist, and no wheaten flour. Twenty years ago the miller employed four assistants, whereas today he has but one, and he usually had fifteen hundred sacks of wheat shot out loose in the great loft waiting to run through the stones that turned night and day, grinding the golden grain into flour for use about the near countryside. The walls of the mill are very strongly built. The beams within are as large as trees, which was necessary to enable them to carry such a great weight of corn and plant.

The large 'under-shot' wheel that turns the stones is half of iron and half of wood. The beautiful water sings sweetly as its task, and the tame trout come close up to the mill-head and thrust their

ARLINGTON MILL, BIBURY

noses against the iron grating, as though curious to see the wheel at work and to know what is going on within the cavern-like place.

SQUIRREL PIE

The men of Fairford were skilled in the use of flails, and they travelled for many miles during the winter months, threshing out wheat and barley. When the machine threshers were invented the lively Coln was harnessed to the toil and threshed out the corn as well as grinding flour for the loaves. The Fairford horse-threshing teams also traversed the country around for a great distance. Four horses, attached to as many levers, supplied the power for the thresher. They were outside the barn, while the machine was set within. In the centre, from which the levers radiated, was a cage in which a boy stood to drive the animals; there he must stay in rain or snow, ofttimes drenched to the skin, and half-perished with the cold.

'Many's the time I squat in that owl' cage an' drev thasy 'osses round,' the aged carter says.

'Warn thees jest about fancied thiself, dissent?' his wife replies, with a sly wink and a knowing nod of the head.

But there were hard times around Fairford and in the Cotswold villages during the 'Hungry Forties', and the poor found it difficult to subsist even on the rudest fare. With wheaten flour at a prohibitive price and barley meal costing a guinea a bushel, what were the labouring classes to do? Yet live they must, and it is not to be wondered at if they took to poaching and stole a sheep now and then in order to satisfy the raging hunger within them. Hedgehogs were a common article of food. Badgers, also, were eagerly hunted and devoured, and the nimble squirrel was frequently trapped, cooked and eaten by the woodmen and labourers. The local squire was surprised at the carter's eating a squirrel. He thought the dish to be unclean, but the carter grinned broadly and replied: 'Aa, zur, you don' know the vally of a squirrel. Tha be as dainty mate as ever you tasted, an' good anuff for the king to aat.'

BIBURY, LOOKING TOWARDS THE VILLAGE

BIBURY, LOOKING TOWARDS ARLINGTON

A COTSWOLD OX TEAM

THE CARTER'S TALES

It was the practice, on New Year's Day, for all the ploughmen to come home from the field at noon and stable their horses. Then the head carter, carrying the plough spanner and a wooden wedge in his hand, and followed by the under ploughman and boys, proceeded to the kitchen, and laid them on the table before the mistress with the remark, 'Now for the owl' cock, Missis!'

After that the carter and his mates went outside and chased the cock round the farmyard for ten or fifteen minutes and then came into the kitchen and sat down to a substantial meal. There was no more ploughing that day. The afternoon was spent in the stables, cleaning the harness. On the morrow they went out, stronger and braver, to plough the regulation acre, provided the weather and land were favourable.

At one place where the carter worked as a boy the old farmer was very eccentric. When harvest-home came round one year and the fires were burning brightly in the brewhouse and beneath the big copper boiler, he peeped through the shutters and was astonished to see the master throw an old pair of boots into the boiler among the meat and vegetables. Accordingly, when supper-time came and all the men were busy at table, he alone would not touch anything, but pretended to be sick, and lay on the ground during the meal. The next day he told the men what he had seen, and they gave him a good thrashing for not speaking about it earlier.

At another time a teamster came home, with a load of ashes, the worse for liquor. Thereupon the farmer scolded him for his indulgence. Nettled by the master's remarks, the carter seized the bridle, led the horse quickly into the narrow barn, turned the wagon round sharply, and came out again.

'Yellock! Thee coussent do that,' said he.

'No more coussent thee, if tha hassent bin drunk,' the other replied.

Old Ambrose Archer, of Quenington, had three hoes which he used according to the price he was being paid for the job. One of these was for 2s. 6d. an acre, one for 3s., and the other for 5s. an acre.

COTTAGE AT LILFIELD, NEAR STROUD

'Good morning, David! Raw air this morning!' said the visitor to a rustic.

'Aa, 'tis, you! Dwun suppose a bin biled awhever,' he replied.

And again: 'Fine morning John!'

'Marnin's all right ef thee't let un alone!'

So also with the farmer who addressed the labourer one cold winter's morning:

'Mornin', James! Fine mornin', James!'

'Fine marnin's no good wi' no bren cheese in the cubberd, maester,' James answered. –

A villager was going to the workhouse to obtain relief there, when someone addressed him:

'Good morning, Etherd!'

'Oy! Oy! I'm a-gwoin on yander. Some on 'em got girt sticks in ther faggots, but I got none in mine,' replied he, meaning some people had meat in their broth, but he had none in his.

One day a travelling salt, on his way from Gloucester to London, was taking a short cut across farmer B—'s field. When he was half-way over the farmer galloped up behind him and cried:

"Owld on! Ther's no road yer acraas my land.'

'Oh! Thy land is it? And how comes it to be thy land?' said the salt.

"Twas left to ma hi mi faather,' the farmer answered.

'And how did he come by 't?' the sailor enquired.

"Ad it from 'es foorefaathers afore 'e.'

'And where did they get it?'

'Why! fowt for 't, 'e s'pose,' the farmer replied.

'Very good! If thee't get off that 'oss I'll fight thee for 't, but I shan't go hack for nobody,' the salt answered.

THE CARTER'S BOYS

THE CARTER'S COTTAGE

The carter's cottage may be held as a fair type of the average home of the Cotswold labourer. The house is of moderate size, with two rooms downstairs and two above. One of the downstairs rooms is set aside as a summer apartment, for when the sun shines hot against the front of the house the temperature within is raised to an uncomfortable pitch.

The other is the general living-room, constituting dining- and sitting-room and kitchen together. The furniture of the room consists of a large deal table, an ancient sofa covered with faded red cloth, a chest of drawers, and half a dozen chairs, including the armchair by the fireside, in which no one else must presume to sit when the carter is at home. Standing within the door is an old-fashioned oak folding table, the envy of dealers who pass by, who constantly make advances to the carter's wife and implore her to sell it, but to no purpose.

'Do you want to get rid o' that owl' table, mother?' the dealers ask.

'No. Shan't seel 'e. 'E's years an' years ow 'e is, if anybody knowed the ins an' outs o' that owld table. Ther'd be jest about a 'ow d 'e do if I was to get rid on in. 'E was left to mine bi 'e's grandmother, an' I knows 'e'll never pert wi'n,' she replies.

As usual in a poor man's cottage, what is lacking in furniture is made up for in pictures and ornaments. There are no less than fifty ornaments on the mantelpiece. They are of all sorts and dimensions, but are chiefly old-fashioned stone figures and pieces of quaint chinaware, many of them interesting, and some highly valuable. Foremost among them are two fine old images of Tom King and Dick Turpin, the robbers, which the dealers have often tried in vain to buy; the modest sum of eleven shillings for the two was not enough to tempt the carter's wife to sell them.

As with ornaments, so with pictures and photographs; there are nearly a hundred hanging upon the walls of the living-room. Of these the most conspicuous are a reproduction of *The Stolen Duchess*, in colours, and two old scriptural prints – *The Finding of Moses* and *Moses in the Land of Midian*. The

THE CARTER, HORSES AND BOY

mirror, before which the carter has his weekly shave, is marked with the name of a certain embrocation, warranted 'Good for Cattle', and the covering over the back of the good-wife's chair is a piece of
hand-wrought embroidery depicting Joseph's flight with the infant Christ into Egypt. Hanging up are a
hempen halter and a great horn lantern for use in the stables; upon the floor are a long brass-handled
whip and a flag dinner basket.

The carter is a strong-made man, with broad shoulders, short, thick neck, massive head, and square face,
and he has a loud, deep voice, just the kind to terrify the ploughboys when they have been guilty of any
misdemeanour. His wife is a portly dame, honest and homely, whose chief pride is in keeping a clean house
and having everything ready for her 'man' when he comes home at meal-times and in the evening.

Their family is twelve in number – six sons and six daughters – though they are all grown up and
away from home now. Of the sons one is a sailor, three are soldiers, and the other a railwaymen. The
daughters are either married or in situations, and do not come home very often. As neither the carter
nor his wife can read or write there is little correspondence between them. The eldest son writes once a
year – at Christmas; then they get one of the neighbours to come in and read it to them and write out a
reply. Yet in spite of many hardships suffered during a laborious life, the carter is bright and cheerful,
and is able to tell a merry tale and recount several quaint customs of which he had heard his father
speak, but which have been discontinued of late years.

Alfred Williams

COTSWOLD WOMEN

The Cotswold women obtain employment in the fields at certain seasons of the year; though poorly
paid, they are usually more conscientious and hard-working than the men.

Most of their cottages are kept scrupulously clean; they have an air of homely comfort which calls
forth the admiration of all strangers. The children, too, when they go to church on Sundays, are dressed

THE CARTER'S TEAMS

with a neatness and good taste that are simply astonishing when one recalls the income of a labourer on the Cotswolds – seldom, alas! averaging more than fourteen shillings a week. A boy of twelve years of age is able to keep himself, earning about five shillings per week. Cheerful and manly little chaps they are. To watch a boy of fourteen years of age managing a couple of great strong cart-horses, either at the plough or with the wagons, is a sight to gladden the heart of man.

THE PREMATURE ARRIVAL

As to the morals of the Gloucestershire peasants in general; and of our village in particular, it may be said that they are on the whole excellent; in one respect only they are rather casual, not to say prehistoric.

The following story gives one a very good idea of the casual nature of hamlet morals:

A parson – I do not know of which village, but it was somewhere in this neighbourhood – paid a visit to a newly married man, to speak seriously about the exceptionally premature arrival of an heir. 'This is a terrible affair,' said the parson on entering the cottage. 'Yaas; 'twere a bad job to be sure,' replied the man. 'And what will yer take to drink?'

Let it in justice be said that such episodes are the exception and not the rule.

FIGHTING BY CANDLELIGHT

Sense of humour of a kind the Cotswold labourer certainly has, even though he is quite unable to see a large number of apparently simple jokes. The diverting history of John Gilpin, for instance, read at a smoking concert, was received with scarce a smile.

Old Mr Peregrine lately told me of an instance of the extraordinary secretiveness of the labourer. Two of his men worked together in his barn day after day for several weeks. During that time they never spoke to each other, save that one of them would always say the last thing at night, 'Be sure to shut the door.'

Oddly enough they thoroughly appreciate the humour of the wonderful things that went on fifty and a hundred years ago. The old farmer I have just mentioned told me that he remembers when he used to go to church fifty years ago, how, after they had all been waiting half an hour, the clerk would pin a notice in the porch, 'No church today; Parson C. got the gout.'

As with history so also with geography, the Cotswold labourer sometimes gets 'a bit mixed'.

''Ow be they a-gettin on in Durbysher?' lately enquired a man at Coln St Aldwyns.

To him replied a righteously indignant native of the same village, 'I've 'eard as 'ow the English army 'ave killed ten thousand Durvishera [Dervishes].'

'Begad!' answered his friend, 'there won't be many left in Durbysher if they goes on a-killin' un much longer.'

Another story lately told me in the same village was as follows. An old lady went to the stores to buy candles, and was astonished to find that owing to the Spanish-American war 'candles was riz'.

'Get along!' she indignantly exclaimed. 'Don't tell me they fights by candlelight.'

THE CARTER'S FECUNDITY

One of the cheeriest fellows that ever worked for us was a carter called Trinder. He was the father of twenty-one children – by the same wife. He never seemed to be worried in the slightest degree by domestic affairs, and was always happy and healthy. This man's wages would be about twelve shillings a week: not a very large sum for a man with a score of children. Then it must be remembered that the boys would go off to work in the fields at a very early age, and by the time they were ten years old they would be keeping themselves. A large family like this would not have the crushing effect on the labouring man that it has on the poor curate or city clerk. Nevertheless, one cannot help looking upon the man as a kind of hero, when one considers the enormous number of grandchildren and descendants he will have. On being asked the other day how he had contrived to maintain such a quiverful, he answered, 'I've always managed to get along all right so far; I never wanted for vittals, sir, anyhow.' This was all the information he would give.

AN INSTRUMENT OF GOOD

One old man being asked why he liked the vicar made answer as follows: 'Why, 'cos he be so scratchy after sould.' The same man lately said to the parson, 'Sir, you be an instrument of good in this place.'

This old-fashioned Cotswold man was very fond of reciting long passages out of Psalms: indeed, he knew half the Prayer-book by heart; and one day the hearer, being rather wearied, exclaimed, 'I must go now, for it's my dinner-time.' To whom replied the old man, 'Oh! be off with thee, then; thee thinks more of thee belly than thee God.'

An old bedridden woman was visited by the parson, and the following dialogue took place:

'Well, Annie, how are you today?'

'O sir, I be so bad! My inside be that comical I don't know what to do with he; he be all on the ebb and flow.'

The same clergyman knew an old Cotswold labourer who wished to get rid of the evil influence of the Devil. So Hodge wrote a polite, though firm, epistle, telling his Satanic Majesty he would have no more to do with him. On being asked where he posted his letter, he replied 'A' dug a hole i' the ground, and popped un in there. He got it right enough, for he's left me alone from that day to this.'

BURFORD

HORSE-BUS TO BURFORD

Burford and Cirencester are two typical Cotswold towns; and perhaps the first-named is the most characteristic, as it is also the most remote and old-world of all places in this part of England. It was on a lovely day in June that I resolved to go and explore the ancient priory and glorious church of old Burford. A very slow train set me down at Bampton, commonly called Bampton-in-the-Bush, though the forest which gave rise to the name has long since given place to open fields.

I was fortunate enough to secure an outside seat on the rickety old 'bus' which plies between Bampton and Burford, and was soon slowly traversing the white limestone road, stopping every now and then to set down a passenger or deposit a parcel at some clean-looking, stone-faced cottage in the straggling old villages.

It was indeed a glorious morning for an expedition into the Cotswolds. Six weeks' drought had just given place to cool, showery weather. A light wind from the west breathed the fragrance of countless wild flowers and sweet may blossom from the leafy hedges, and the scent of roses and honeysuckle was wafted from every cottage garden. After a month spent amid the languid air and depressing surroundings of London, one felt glad at heart to experience once again the grand, pure air and rural scenery of the Cotswold Hills.

What strikes one so forcibly about this part of England, after a sojourn in some smoky town, is its extraordinary cleanliness.

There is no such thing as dirt in a limestone country. The very mud off the roads in rainy weather is not dirt at all, sticky though it undoubtedly is. It consists almost entirely of lime, which, though it burns all the varnish off your carriage if allowed to remain on it for a few days, has nothing repulsive about its nature like ordinary mud.

BURFORD HIRING FAIR

THE HIRING FAIR

One of the old institutions which still remain in the Cotswolds is the annual 'mop', or hiring fair. At Cirencester these take place twice in October. Every labouring man in this district hurries into the town, where all sorts of entertainments are held in the market-place, including 'whiny-go-rounds', discordant music, and the usual 'shows' which go to make up a country fair. 'Hiring' used to be the great feature of these fairs. In the days before local newspapers were invented every sort of servant, from a farm bailiff to a maid-of-all-work, was hired for the year at the annual mop. The word 'mop' is derived from an old custom which ordained that the maid-servants who came to find situations should bring their badge of office with them to the fair. They came with their brooms and mops, just as a carter would tie a piece of whipcord to his coat, and a shepherd's hat would be decorated with a tuft of wool. Time was when the labouring man was never happy unless he changed his abode from year to year. He would get tired of one master and one village, and be off to Cirencester mop, where he was pretty sure to get a fresh job. But nowadays the Cotswold men are beginning to realise that 'Two removes are as bad as a fire.' The best of them stay for years in the same village. This is very much more satisfactory for all concerned. Deeply rooted though the love of change appears to be in the hearts of nine-tenths of the human race, the restless spirit seldom enjoys real peace and quiet; and the discontent and poverty of the labouring class in times gone by may safely be attributed to their never-ceasing changes and removal of their belongings to other parts of the country.

Now that these old fairs no longer answer the purpose for which they existed for hundreds of years, they will doubtless gradually die out. And they have their drawbacks. An occasion of this kind is always associated with a good deal of drunkenness; the old market-place of Cirencester for a few days in each autumn becomes a regular pandemonium. It is marvellous how quickly all traces of the great show are swept away and the place once more settles down to the normal condition of an old-fashioned though well-to-do country town.

J. Arthur Gibbs

LABOURERS AND THREE HORSE TEAMS

MOTHER

Our grandfather retired from his horses and went into the liquor business. He became host at The Plough, a small Sheepscombe ion, and when Grandmother died, a year or two afterwards, Mother left service to help him. Those were days of rough brews, penny ales, tuppenny rums, home made cider, the staggers, and violence. Mother didn't altogether approve of the life, but she entered the calling with spirit. 'That's where I learned the frog-march,' she'd say; 'and there were plenty of those who got it! Pug Sollars, for instance; the biggest bully in Sheepscombe – cider used to send him mad. He'd pick up the tables and lay about him like an animal while the chaps hid behind the piano. "Annie!" they'd holler, "for the Lord's sake save us!" I was the only one could handle Pug. Many's the time I've caught him by the collar and run him along the passage. Others, too – if they made me wild, I'd just throw them out in the road. Dad was too easy, so it was me had to do it. . . . They smirk when they see me now.'

The Plough Inn was built as one of the smaller stages on the old coach road to Birdlip; but by Mother's time the road had decayed and was no longer the main route to anywhere. One or two carters, impelled by old habits, still used the lane and the inn, and Mother gave them ale and bacon suppers and put them to sleep in the stables. Otherwise, few travellers passed that way, and the lane was mostly silent. So through the long afternoons Mother fell into dreams of idleness, would dress in her best and sit out on the terrace, reading, or copying flowers. She was a lonely young woman, mysteriously detached, graceful in face and figure. Most of the village boys were afraid of her, of her stormy temper, her superior wit, her unpredictable mental exercises.

Mother spent several odd years in that village pub, living her double life, switching from bar-room rages to terrace meditations, and waiting while her twenties passed. Grandfather, on the other hand, spent his time in the cellars playing the fiddle across his boot. He held the landlordship of an inn to be the same as Shaw's definition of marriage – as something combining the maximum of temptation with the maximum of opportunity. So he seldom appeared except late in the evening, when he'd pop

THE FORD, SHIPTON OLIFFE

up through a hole in the floor, his clothes undone, his face streaming with tears, singing 'The Warrior's Little Boy'.

Mother stuck by him faithfully, handled the drunks, grew older, and awaited deliverance. Then one day she read in a local paper: 'Widower (4 children) Seeks Housekeeper.'

She had had enough of Pug Sollars by now, and of fiddle-tunes in the cellar. She changed into her best, went out on the terrace, sat down, and answered the advertisement. A reply came back, an appointment was made; and that's how she met my father.

When she moved into his tiny house in Stroud, and took charge of his four small children, Mother was thirty and still quite handsome. She had not, I suppose, met anyone like him before. This rather priggish young man, with his devout gentility, his airs and manners, his music and ambitions, his charm, bright talk, and undeniable good looks, overwhelmed her as soon as she saw him. So she fell in love with him immediately, and remained in love for ever. And herself being comely, sensitive, and adoring, she attracted my father also. And so he married her. And so later he left her – with his children and some more of her own.

When he'd gone she brought us to the village and waited. She waited for thirty years. I don't think she ever knew what had made him desert her, though the reasons seemed clear enough. She was too honest, too natural for this frightened man; too remote from his tidy laws. She was, after all, a country girl; disordered, hysterical, loving. She was muddled and mischievous as a chimney-jackdaw, she made her nest of rags and jewels, was happy in the sunlight, squawked loudly at danger, pried and was insatiably curious, forgot when to eat or ate all day, and sang when sunsets were red. She lived by the easy laws of the hedgerow, loved the world, and made no plans, had a quick holy eye for natural wonders and couldn't have kept a neat house for her life. What my father wished for was something quite different, something she could never give him – the protective order of an unimpeachable suburbia, which was what he got in the end.

The three or four years Mother spent with my father she fed on for the rest of her life. Her happiness

MICKLETON

at that time was something she guarded as though it must ensure his eventual return. She would talk about it almost in awe, not that it had ceased but that it had happened at all.

'He was proud of me then. I could make him laugh. "Nance, you're a killer," he'd say. He used to sit on the doorstep quite helpless with giggles at the stories and things I told him. He admired me too; he admired my looks; he really loved me, you know. "Come on, Nance," he'd say. "Take out your pins. Let your hair down – let's see it shine!" He loved my hair; it had gold lights in it then and it hung right down my back. So I'd sit in the window and shake it over my shoulders – it was so heavy you wouldn't believe – and he'd twist and arrange it so that it caught the sun, and then sit and just gaze and gaze.

'Sometimes, when you children were all in bed, he'd clear all his books away – "Come on, Nance," he'd say, "I've had enough of them. Come and sing us a song!" We'd go to the piano, and I'd sit on his lap, and he'd play with his arms around me. And I'd sing him "Killarney" and "Only a Rose". They were both his favourites then.

When she told us these things it was yesterday

CHEDWORTH

CLUB DAY AT EBRINGTON

and she held him again in her enchantment. His later scorns were stripped away and the adored was again adoring. She'd smile and look up the weed-choked path as though she saw him coming back for more.

Laurie Lee

A DEAD SHEEP

One evening while returning home I met a man who'd been a shepherd the greater part of his life, but who, having been able to save sufficient money to take a few odd fields, was now busily engaged in losing his small accumulation.

'How goes it today, shepherd?' I said.

'Oh, Master John, 'tis you, is 't? I be right glad to see 'ee, 'tis some time since I 'ad a sight on 'ee. Why, things is but middling, yer know, an' there's one o' th 'ow yeows a bit middling today.'

'Oh! that's a bad job; will you have to kill her, do you think?'

'I most expects I shall; 'er doan't sim to mend none an' I means fur to be in time wi' thic un. One time just arter I'd begun to kip a feaw ship on m' own account, one o' the tegs wur a-took middling. Wall, I said to myself, thee sims bad-like, but p'raps thee'lt git auver it. Onyways I 'ont gie thee a drunch, vur ef so be I should 'a to kill th', 'twud spile the mate. So I let un bide a bit; an' when I comed back to un zome time arterwards, thur didn't sim much odds in un one way nor t'other. I didn't want fur to lose un if I could help it, and didn't want to kill un, if 'er wur like to git roun', yer knaow. Wall, I thought I'd let un have another chance, an' I'd come and see to un agin pretty soon. However, when I comed back to un, dalled if 'er wurn't a-most djed, an' afore I wur able to git out my knife to kill un, 'er'd gone quite off "Bost thy kearcass," I zays to un, "why iver's thee gone an' died afore I killed thee!" Wall, I wasn't able to afford to lose the mate, so I cuts 'ers throat quick, an' as 'er couldn't say baa fur 'erself, I sed baa vor un, in case thur wur ar-a-one a-watching me. Then I teaks un accross the ground, an' when I'd a-hung un up in th' woak tree, I starts fur to git 'ers pelt off', an' to dress un a bit. 'While I wur to work up comes Master Jonas, the butcher.

"Hallo, shepherd," er sed, "what's thee got thur?"

"Oh! just o' a casalty ship," I sed. "I seed 'er wur a bit middlin' like, an' so I took and killed un, not to lose the mate."

BLOCKLEY

"What's a-gwine to do wi' un, shepherd?" er says. "Get shut on un somehow," I says to un; "there's a plenty o' yolk as 'ull buy un, yer knaow."

"What does 'ee want fur un, shepherd, take un as 'er is?"

"A matter o' ten bob," says I.

"Ten bob!" er says, "fur that thur djed ship."

"Djed ship!" I says, "er yain't a djed ship, I just a-bin a' killed un."

"Killed un, 'ave 'ee," er says; "think I can't see as that thur ship wur djed afore you killed un? Look at the mate," er says. "Tell 'ee what I'll do, I'll gie 'ee three bob for un."

"I won't sell," I says.

'Wall, we bided thur and haggled a smart while, and then er says er'd gie I five bob if I'd gie un a tanner out for luck; but I 'oodn't.

"Don't 'ee be so 'nation hard in the mouth," er says; "gie a body a chance to make an honest living."

'Wall, at last as I bided firm er gied I a matter o' three half-crownds fur un, an' I gied un a bob out for luck.

"An' what'll 'ee do wi' un, Master Jonas?" says I. "Do wi' un?" er says, "why, put un straight away into my trap, an' that thur as th' inspector don't see I'll sell out to the yolks, an' th' rest on't shall go round th' townd to th' ow maids for cats' vittles," er sed; that's what er'd do wi' et.'

S.S. Bucknsan

FORTHAMPTON

KINGSCOURT, STROUD

THE GLEANERS

The village schools were always closed for gleaning. This was the harvest holidays. Nearly all the village wives turned out, and the children went, too. We took the day's provisions in a bag, and a cup to dip the water from the little spring bubbling up under the hazels, with a clean white sheet, or counterpane, taken from the bed, for the 'nitches', and small linen ear-bags to be fastened round the waist for the loose ears, broken off by the reapers, or more frequently 'britted' off by the heat of the sun. There were always a few to anticipate the general hive, and have the early run of the field, though these frequently fared worst in the end. My mother and we children were usually the last to enter a field and the last to leave it. Our appearance was hailed with a good-natured cheer, and often a little humorous banter, but we always bore off the fattest bundle in the end. We used to consider our harvest a poor one if it did not total fifteen or sixteen bushels of threshed grain.

There were eight of us altogether – my mother and six others – ranging from five to thirteen years. All the children gathered small handfuls, then brought them to her; she put them together into one, twisted a part of the straw round several times, and thrust the ends underneath the bond, then set it down in the stubble, ears up, and went on as before. In the morning we had lunch at ten, dinner at noon, with 'little dinner' again in the afternoon, about four. We went home about six or seven, telling the time by the sun. Perhaps we gathered forty large handfuls, or perhaps less, according to the quantity of ears on the ground. We always gleaned more in dull weather; then we could see the ears better. At night, after reaching home, all the ears were cut off with a sharp knife or scissors, and then stored in sacks and kept indoors. The cottage was like a little barn, upstairs and down, too; you could scarcely move for the corn.

EARLY TO BED, EARLY TO RISE

The village people retire early, and the farmers before the work-folk, as a rule. A great many of the farmers retire at eight, and even by seven, in the winter, after partaking of a good supper of bread and

CHALFORD

cheese, and hotted beer, or cider – wives, daughters and all. Before retiring the farmer usually takes a lantern and walks round the cattle-yard and stables, to see that everything is safe and well. Very often the farm-labourers are much later in going to bed, burning the oil till eleven and after; but this is a bad sign. In the villages farther from the town they retire much earlier.

The villagers' food, especially that of the labouring class, is plain and simple in kind, but plentiful enough. The chief article consumed is bread, and abundant potatoes; where there is a large family of six or eight, the household requires eight or nine gallons of bread a week, or more, and then the wife and mother cooks potatoes for dinner and tea as well. The chief trimmings are Canadian bacon and cheese, butter or margarine, lard or dripping. The children eat bread and lard, with pepper upon it.

Bacon-pudding is a tasty meal, though waning in favour. The old carter may have a fried rasher – without the egg – for breakfast, or fried vegetables, or toasted cheese. Fresh meat is only indulged in once a week, Sundays. That is generally purchased from the van which comes round every Saturday – breast or loin of mutton, or brisket of beef – and is mostly foreign, though some country labourers will not touch the 'furren tackle', and abhor all tinned goods. A short while ago a dealer was selling sausages in the village at threepence a pound, best fourpence. The carter's wife did not like the former kind: 'They burned their mouths so, and made the children cry awful.' At Christmas all the labourers receive a large piece of prime beef, from eight to twelve pounds, and very many a ton of coal at Michaelmas, besides a sum of money. Their drink consists chiefly of tea, very weak – this they have three and very often four times a day – and many keep a small barrel of ale in the house, too, or else fetch it from the inn.

Alfred Williams

RUFUS CLAY

One evening as I was walking down the road with Thesiger Crowne we passed a long-striding, heavily bearded man, wearing a slouch hat, baggy coat and trousers, and shabby black leggings falling well

COLN ST ALDWYN

down on to his boots. He was carrying a gun, and beside him trotted a large retriever dog. I had not seen him before.

'Who is that?' I enquired of Thesiger.

'Rufus Clay,' he answered. 'He's a foreigner.'

Signs of red hair at birth may have encouraged his parents to call him Rufus, but it certainly turned out to be a misnomer. His full beard was black, and his complexion swarthy, but I thought the man looked English.

'A foreigner? What is he – a Spaniard?'

'Spaniard?' said Thesiger. 'No. He come from Pinswick.'

'You mean he lives there?'

'No. He do not live there. He do live here.'

Pinswick is a village seventeen miles away, on the other side of the county. I was puzzled.

'But you said he was a foreigner.'

'Yes, he be a foreigner. He's a Pinswicker.'

'But how long has he lived here?' I persisted.

'Oh, not above ten or twelve years.'

I had been Thesiger's neighbour for eighteen months, and I came from five counties away. As he spoke, I supposed that he must look upon me as something out of the sea at least, though we always seemed to be very good friends. I discovered that nothing short of two generations of unbroken tenure constitutes native rights. Settlers, if only from the next parish, are foreigners, and openly called so. For casual pass-the-time-of-day acquaintance, even for neighbourly talk, this is no particular disability, but if you come with the intention of carrying on business, you are likely to be disillusioned, as Rufus Clay learnt.

A few days later I found his house. It was buried behind high walls, not visible from the road. There was nothing mysterious about it, but unless you had special occasion to go in, it was out of sight and out of mind. Rufus had set up as a cobbler, coming to the place when he was between forty

NORTH NIBLEY

and fifty, with a small bag full of savings. On a broken board over the wall door was written, 'Rufus Clay. Cobbler. Repairs neatly executed.' But in a month he found that for trade he might as suitably have gone to a city of the dead. Why he had stayed on for ten years nobody enquired, and he himself did not seem to know. I was told that he had a large kitchen garden, and sold some of the produce on the rare occasions when anybody wanted to buy. I went in now and found him digging. I asked him if he could let me have some onions. He looked at me without saying anything, did not move for a few moments, then stuck his fork into the ground, and pulled up as many onions as he could hold by the tops in two large hands, and gave them to me.

'How much?' I asked.

'Oh, a penny.'

'Only a penny'

'Is doesn't master. Tuppence if you like.'

I paid him, sorry that he had not asked more. As he put the coppers into his pocket, he remarked, 'You're a foreigner too, aren't you?' He said it a little sadly, with a touch of bitterness.

'I suppose they would call me that,' I answered.

'Yes, they would. Unnatural I call it.'

THE WOOD MANOR HOUSE

'Don't you get on with the folk here?' I ventured.

'Get on – how the darnation can you get on? I don't know them, and they don't know me. Never will. It isn't civilized.'

'You've been here a good many years now, haven't you?'

'Eleven years too long,' was the reply. 'I'm a gowk to have stuck it.'

I asked him to have some tobacco, which he did. I wondered why he had stayed so long if he did not like it. It seemed that in the winter epidemic of 19— he had lost his wife and two children at a stroke, and had left Painswick forever. He had settled down into his new quarters not hopefully, but without misgiving. The prejudice against 'foreigners' had surprised him. He had not spirit to fight it, nor heart to move on. So that with his few pence saved and the help of a garden he had drifted along in a sullen but not actively resentful lethargy.

While we were talking, the retriever that had been on the road with him that evening lay on the earth among a not very prosperous crop of cabbages, at full stretch in the sun. He had taken no notice of my arrival, but as I bade Rufus good-day and turned to go he was at my side in an instant, spiny-furred and growling. His master called him to heel, and as he did so the affection in his voice was clear. It was the first sign he had given of any sustaining human warmth. 'He's ten years old. He's all I've got,' he said. 'Him and high walls.'

I found in the village that there was no antagonism towards Rusus Clay. He just didn't exist. What might have happened if he had been the sort to persevere in advances I can't say. After the first month or two of failure he had made none, and for all the thought he was given he might as well have been within the churchyard walls as his own. Now and again I went to him on some small marketing errand, and once in a while I would meet him on the road at nightfall, his gun on arm, and his one friend behind him. I never heard his name mentioned but once. On a late August evening in the Chippendale Arms there was a meeting to start the local football club on its way for the coming season. There was some difficulty in getting a sufficient number of willing and eligible people to serve on the committee. During a lull a youth, for want of something likelier to suggest, said, 'What about Mr Clay?' There was a rustle of disapproval, and I thought I heard a murmur of 'foreigner' from the corner where the chairman, the Chippendale Arms host, was sitting. No other notice was taken of the question.

Then once again his name was spoken. Late in the following spring Thesiger Crowne, Tom Benton, Isaac Putcher, Rawson Leaf, and myself with some others were standing by a gate at the village end, gossiping of nothing in particular. Beyond the gate a path ran some three-quarters of a mile, straight down through four meadows, to the bank of a derelict canal. A few yards along the bank to the right could he seen a disused lock. As we were talking, we saw the figure of Rufus Clay in the distance, walking along the bank with his dog, towards the path. No attention was paid until they reached the lock side. Then the retriever came to a sudden halt, barked excitedly, and in a moment disappeared over the side. We could see the man's agitation even at that distance, but still the talk was hardly interrupted. Then a strange thing happened. Rufus stood upright a moment, seemed to quiver, and plunged after his friend. At once we were in full flight down the field. It was too late. What had drawn the dog in, whether a rat or what else, no one knew. But the lock with its water fifteen feet below bank level, was a death trap. Both dog and man were past our help. It was an hour before they could be got out. And then Thesiger Crowne said, 'A bad job that. Rufus Clay. These foreigners do never learn their way about.'

John Drinkwater

THE LAY PREACHER

I remember one old local preacher, named Maslin, who used to come to the chapel now and then clad in a white smock reaching halfway below the knees. This old fellow was an agricultural labourer. He was

BLOCKLEY

very short in stature, with grey hair, and exceedingly bronzed and sunburnt; he had toiled among
the sheep and lambs, the wheat and oats, and had
heard the lark sing in the blue heavens thousands
of times. He had also felt the cold nipping wind
sweeping up the valley and over the hilltops, and
had trudged through the deep snow to the village
over and over again. When he came to preach he
carried his dinner tied up in a red handkerchief and
hung on a blackthorn stick over his shoulder. His
fare was very simple – bread and cheese, and he
must have a glass of ale with it from somewhere
or other; he did not indulge in hot cooked food
that day. A great number used to go and hear him
preach; he could always command a congregation,
he was so sternly simple, outspoken, and comical.
He was a firm believer in the Devil as a personality.
Once when he had been called to see a sick man,
and had not been able to make a very deep impression on the unfortunate, he attributed it all to the
actual presence of the Evil One. 'I know'd 'a was
ther,' the old man declared most gravely, 'for I could
smell the brimstone; the house was full on't.'

One Sunday evening, in late autumn, he was

A LABOURER FROM BROOKTHORPE

BURFORD STREET, LECHLADE

down to preach, and there was the usual full attendance; the little chapel was packed; a great time was expected; they were not all disappointed. Old Maslin was beside himself, and preached vehemently. As the sermon proceeded – it was half sermon and half prayer – he waxed hotter and hotter. Now he leaned far forwards over the rails of the pulpit, now jumped backward, stamped hard with his feet, and swayed from side to side. The congregation perspired, and trembled in their pews. Louder and louder the old fellow's voice pealed out; he stamped harder and harder; everyone felt something was to happen, and happen it did. There was a large iron stove in that chapel; it stood in the centre. The pipes from this went up and then passed horizontally to the wall some distance away. Moreover, they had not been swept out for a long time, and were become very foul. The storm raged with increasing fury. The old folk were getting uncomfortable; the young girls tittered. The preacher shouted at the top of his voice, and stamped mightily with his feet. 'Send the power, and send it now!' he cried. One more moment, and it came. The joints of the pipes could stand no longer. With a shuddering crack the whole lot of the horizontals toppled down. A loud yell went up from the people, the youth exploded, but there were no heads broken. There was a prompt young man sitting just underneath that pipe. At the first crack he leapt up and caught it falling; but he made a sinister use of the opportunity. Receiving the pipes in the middle, with a dexterous movement of the hands, he twirled them round, and shot vast clouds of soot over all the people from one end of the place to the other. The result may be better imagined than described; it was like a pandemonium. All Maslin's preaching faded beside that night; that was his veritable coup d'éclat. The old man has been dead this quarter of a century.

Alfred Williams

ODD-JOB MAN'S DELIGHT

The place might have been either blackened by belching chimneys or blighted by the withering presence of decrepit colonels drawing out their last meaningless days. Miraculously preserved from both disasters, the little town muddled along contentedly enough in its own haphazard way; and

THE VEGETABLE MAN AT FAIRFORD

although I suppose a very high percentage of the population must have been technically 'unemployed' there was much less poverty and very much less distress than you would find in similar circumstances in an industrial town. The city-dweller, when he is out of work, is generally helpless; there are few 'odd-jobs' to be had, even if he were adaptable enough to be capable of doing them. But in the country and in the country-town it is different; and Elmbury was an odd-job man's paradise. The farmers in the neighbourhood needed casual labour for a dozen seasonal jobs, haymaking, harvest, fruit-picking, turnip-pulling and what not; a man could earn a few shillings and a quart of cider almost any day he'd a mind to. There was drovering, and there was timber-felling, and there was rick-cutting; thatching, ditch-cleaning, and hedging. Many of the Elmbury men could turn their hands to skilled and semi-skilled jobs such as these. But there were more individualist odd jobs too. In those days, if a man knew something about bird-lime and decoys and clap-nets he could catch a dozen linnets or gold-finches on Brockeridge Common in a morning, and be ten shillings the richer when he had caged and sold them. Even the poorest people bred dogs or canaries or pigeons or rabbits in the backyards of their cottages; many worked allotments and kept chickens or pigs as well. Others got their living out of the river, building boats, netting salmon, cutting osiers, dredging sand, setting putcheons for eels. Almost every man and boy, as we have seen, was a devoted fisherman, but almost every one was a still more devoted poacher. There were other ways of catching salmon beside the legitimate nets or the rods of the rich; and there were plenty of people willing to pay half a sovereign for a clean-run fish, no questions asked or answered.

So that was how many of the Elmbury men lived. In the spring they'd do a bit of salmon fishing, fair or foul; haymaking in June; drovering on Saturday (a walk to the neighbouring market and a drink in the pubs afterwards); plum-picking now and then – but this rather as a favour – for a farmer who was known to be free with his cider; illegal forays after mushrooms on misty September mornings; a few days' beating when squire shot his pheasants; blackberrying; eel-catching at the first autumn flood; and the winter spent variously in building a new punt for sale or hire, caulking an old one, mending the salmon nets, pottering up the river after duck (or perhaps an otter whose skin would be worth a pound), ferreting for rabbits, poaching occasional pheasants, collecting

THE APPLE HARVEST

betting-slips for a bookie, or any one of a score of pleasant, profitable, and adventurous ways.

Now the men who lived in this casual way – and there were several hundred of them Out of our population of five thousand – possessed two advantages which were rare enough then and which are almost priceless today; they were independent of employers, and they were not conditioned to believe in the popular fallacy, that work in itself is a virtue. They worked when they wanted to work; and their work was fun. They were, in fact, a sort of privileged class; and their privilege was one which nowadays only a few great artists have. It was fortunate for Elmbury that its population included these few hundred truly free men; they acted as a leaven upon the whole community.

Their independence of employers gave them a vivid individuality. In those days, when sweated labour in the big industrial districts was sapping the vitality of whole populations and turning millions into rather inefficient robots, the men in the country towns were able to preserve their intelligence, their humour, and their pride. They still believed in a vague, undefined something which they called their 'rights'; and for all their poverty, for all the dirt and squalor in which

A CARRIER AT CIRENCESTER

MAKING WITNEY BLANKETS

BLANKET DRYING

PAINSWICK

THE PAINSWICK CLEANING PARTY

COATES, THAMES HEAD 4TH SPRING

many of them lived, they actually believed that they exercised some rights. They may have called themselves, variously, Conservatives, Radicals and Socialists; but I think really they were the last true Liberals. They believed in Freedom without defining it; but they thought it was something to do with saying 'You-be-damned' to all tyrants, great and small.

John Moore

THE VILLAGE IMPOSTER

Every village seems to possess its share of quaint curious people; but I cannot help thinking that our little hamlet has a more varied assortment of oddities than is usually to be met within so small a place.

There is that very common character 'the village imposter'. After having been turned away by half a dozen different farmers because he never did a stroke of work, he manages to get on the sick list at the 'great house'. Long after his ailment has been cured he will be seen daily going up to the manor house for his allowance of meat; somehow or other he 'can't get a job no how'. The fact is, he has got the name of being an idle scoundrel, and no farmer will take him on. It is some time before you are able to find him out; for he goes decidedly lame as he passes you in the village street, he generally manages to persuade you that he is very ill. Like a fool, you take compassion on him, and give him an ounce of 'baccy' and half a crown. For some months he hangs about where he thinks you will be passing, craving a pipe of tobacco; until one day, when you are having a talk with some other honest toiler, he will give you a hint that you are being imposed on.

When a loafer of this son finds that he can get nothing more out of you he moves his family and goods to some other part of the country; he then begins the old game with somebody else, borrowing a sovereign off you for the expense of moving. As for gratitude, he never thinks of it. The other day a man with a 'game leg', who was, in spite of his lameness, a good example of 'the village imposter', in

THE RIVER COLN AT FAIRFORD

taking his departure from our hamlet, gave out 'that there was no thanks due to the big 'ouse for the benefits he had received, for it was writ in the manor parchments, as how he was to have meat three times a week and blankets at Christmas as long as he was out of work'.

HEALTHY, CLEAN AND OLD-FASHIONED

The Cotswold people are, like their country, healthy, bright, clean, and old-fashioned; and the more educated and refined a man may happen to be, the more in touch he will be with them – not because the peasants are half-refined, but simple, honest, god-fearing folk, who mind their own business and have not sought out many inventions. I am referring now to labourers, because the farmers are a totally different class of men. The latter are on the whole an excellent type of what John Bull ought to be. The labouring class, however, still maintain the old characteristics. A primitive people, as often as not they are 'nature's gentlemen'.

J. Arthur Gibbs

THE VILLAGE DOCTOR

Dr Roberson was an excellent shot. For many years he was a member of the London Rifle Brigade and won a silver cup for shooting. He loved his gun and his spaniel dog, and rented Mr Percy Attwood's shoot on the sixty acres adjoining Ashton Wood on the slopes of Bredon Hill where I farmed for thirty years.

What other doctor took his gun to visit patients on his rounds, I wonder. My cousin George, who at that time lived at the Barracks, Kersoe, adjoining Percy Attwood's land, was ill with flu. The doctor arrived and, not waiting for an answer to his knock, walked straight in. George, who was sitting by his fireside, was confronted by the doctor carrying his gun. He looked up from his chair and, still feeling pretty low, said, 'You haven't come to shoot me Doctor?'

KING'S STANLEY

The old doctor's deafness caused many a laugh. 'How are you boy, I brought you into the world over twenty years ago.'

George replied, 'Oh, I'm better, but have a nasty boil on my neck.'

'Let your trousers down,' the doctor said, propping his gun in the corner of George's cottage sitting-room.

'My neck Doctor, MY NECK!' shouted George.

'Ah, a bread poultice with a little salt, as hot as you can bear it and I'll give you a tonic. You are run down my lad.'

The doctor then walked home under the wood, not empty handed, for his gun kept the family in rabbits and game throughout the season.

Fred Archer

AN AMERICAN'S IMPRESSION

In descending the Cotswold hills, I caught, here and there, some enchanting views: little churches perched upon the brows of hillocks, or half buried in the vales; or farmhouses and cottages not less beautifully situated; or the seats of country squires and other gentry, embosomed amid trees, or lifting their chimneys above a few lordly elms. But the charm of all was yet reserved for me; and just after sunset, as we wound around a broad hillside, I came upon a scene at which, it seemed to me, I might have gazed all my life without weariness or satiety. 'Stop stop! where are you driving?' said I, beseeching him to rein up, and let me look for a few minutes on as perfect a picture of English scenery as ever Gainsborough portrayed, all spread before us, without a blemish; its lights and shadows just as an artist would have them, and yet vivid with nature, beyond all that an artist could create. The time was evening, in one of its sweetest effects of sky and atmosphere, cool and calm; the lighter landscape deeply green; the shadows brown and dying into night; the water shining here like burnished steel, and there lying in shade, as darkly liquid as a dark eye in female beauty.

STOW-ON-THE-WOLD

The view was a narrow dell, just below the road, in which stood an old manor-house, ivied to its chimney tops, and encircled by a moat. Some of the most delicate blue was floating thinly from its chimneys into the clear air, and just at hand was peeping, from a dense growth of trees, the belfry of a very tiny church, which seemed to be there only on purpose to complete the picture. Cattle were grazing in the meads, and under a vast and sombre yew tree sat a group of farm-servants shearing the largest sheep of the flock, the wool flaking off upon the green grass like driven snow. While we gazed on this living picture with mute pleasure, the soft notes of a bird added sweet sounds to the enchantment of sight, and I sat, as in a spell, without speaking a word. My friend, who had been laughing at me all day for my enjoyment of what to him were common and unsuggestive objects, fairly gave up at this point, and owned it was a sight to make one in love with life. Even now I have lying before me a letter in which he refers to this view of 'the sheep-shearing', and concludes by the pathetic announcement that the horse to which we were indebted for that day's progress has since been sold to a coach proprietor, and now runs leader from Evesham to Stratford.

So winding down our road amid firs and oaks, and enjoying new beauties at every turn, we came through Charlton Kings into the broad and teeming vale, adorned by modern Cheltenham. It is a noble amphitheatre, to which the bold outline of the Cotswold hills gives dignity, and which abounds with minor charms on every side. I was soon lodged at my friend's, after due introduction to his family, including a visit to the nursery, where some lovely children were allowed to salute me with their innocent kisses, and thus to make me sure of a welcome to their father's house.

A. Cleveland Coxe

THE CAMPDEN SWEEP

The following lines were to be seen over a door in Chipping Campden many years ago:

> John Hunter, Camden, doe live here,
> Sweeps chimbleys clean, and not too dear;
> And if your chimbley be on fire,
> He'll put it out, if you desire.

When in the town last summer (1882), I failed to discover Hunter's board; but he has evidently had a successor in the business, who has put out a revised edition:

> William Clayton does live here,
> Sweeps chimneys clean, and is not dear;
> And if your chimney is on fire,
> He'll put it out, if you desire.

H.C.W. Gloucestershire Notes & Queries

A GREAT ACQUISITION

On the evenings of Wednesday and Thursday, 23rd and 24th of February, the Stow Amateur Dramatics Society gave an entertainment at the Unicorn Assembly Room which was crowded on both occasions by a very respectable and appreciative audience. The pieces presented were *Luke the Labourer* and *Slasher and Crasher*. There was a marked improvement in the acting upon that of last season, particularly in that of Mr Crannage, as Luke the Labourer; Messrs Goodman and Hopkins, as Slasher and Crasher, were very amusing. Mr Knock is a great acquisition to the society, but we think his performance would be more effective if it were more quiet.

The Gloucester Journal

MORE OF 'SLASHER AND CRASHER'

30 DECEMBER

Party charades at the Hyetts at Painswick. Francis Hyett, Mr Dickinson, Miss Wolley, Mr Walace and Miss Hyett acted Slasher and Crasher, a very amusing play; but the finest fun was in an exhibition of automation wax works, the Marquis of Lorne and Princess Louise kissing hands especially good, and Miss Wolley's singing a Chinese song accompanying herself on a banjo infinitely amusing.

John Dearman Birchall

A SWEET LITTLE COUPLE

> I travelled one day thro' the rain and the cold,
> From the gay streets of London to Stow-on-the-Wold,
> And I sighed to myself, 'twill be dreary and cold,
> A regular desert at Stow-on-the-Wold.

KEMBLE BRIDGE

But a sweet little couple I happened to meet,
Trudging on hand in hand, down the long village street,
And I own that it 'need' not be dreary or cold
At the veriest desert like Stow-on-the-Wold.

H.C.W. Gloucestershire Notes & Queries

THE MASON

Leaning with arms folded upon his garden gate, by which hardly anybody ever passed, Thesiger Crowne
bade me good evening. His cottage was in a bylane of a village that is in itself in an undiscovered
pocket of the Cotswolds. He was a widow man, as they say, and one elderly daughter lived with him.
He looked very handsome this evening. He had a stout frame, tall, and he was rather a dandy, with the
dandy's proper respect for natural tradition. He was a yeoman villager some generations deep, and he
would have scorned to confuse his class with any other. He had been into the market town today, so
that his dress was as it might be on Sunday, with a lay touch of difference. His boots were of the sort in
which he had years ago learnt to walk as many miles as might be, daily in all weathers. His corduroy
trousers, originally buff in colour, had been bleached by repeated washings. Over his cotton shirt, set off
by a linen collar with no tie, in place of a coat be wore a sleeved waistcoat, the sleeves of lining cloth,
the rest of a dark honey-coloured velveteen. His very white hair and whiskers surrounded a very red
face, ample but well shaped, and, as though to remind some of us who play at being countrymen what
the real thing is, he wore a hard black bowler bat of rather fashionable shape.

'Good evening, Mr Crowne,' I replied. 'I hope you're well.'

'Well, that I baint so much. The indigestion it is. I do have often to sit up in bed of a night.' I com-
miserated with him. I asked him if he had seen a doctor.

'Doctors – no. I've made a shift to do without they so far, and that's a deal of time. It's a rest I do
want. If I live, I shall be seventy-seven come Ciceter Mop. I've done a deal of hard work in my time, and
I think it be about time for I to take a rest. Not that I should be surprised, mark you, if I did live to be a

THE BURNT PEST HOUSE

hundred and two.' Presumably the record for the village was held at present by a hundred and one.

A deal of hard work in his time. He was a mason, one of the old Cotswold breed, and his handiwork is in every town and village within twenty miles of the hamlet that had been his home for seventy-seven years. Even beyond that, for the builders recognized his skill, and he had been known to travel on his trade into the further midlands, into Sussex, once even far across into Norfolk. At sixty-six, he told me, he had had a job that for eighteen weeks meant a six-mile walk in the morning, a day's work, and six miles home at night. He had never been out of England, and I talked to him a little of foreign countries. 'Did you ever go to China, sir?' Thesiger had a gift of irony. I had to confess that I had not been there. 'It must be a rare place, China. But no man can go everywhere. That's how I look at it.'

He had a grandson living in the village, one who had fallen from the high craft of masonry to miscellaneous jobbing. Thesiger remembered that when he himself was a boy he used to go with his father to work in a nearby town. His own wages were sixpence a week, and his father drew seven shillings, a considerable share of which was paid in kind – pig's fry and chitlings. He remembered his mother washing them at the spring and selling them to people on the spot. Now his grandson, born and bred in the same place, had been asked for an estimate for whitewashing four cottage rooms. No painting or other work was to be done. His estimate was nineteen pounds. Hearing of the prices that were being paid, he had lost his head and estimated wildly, it is true. But nineteen pounds for, at most, three days' work, and his great grandfather sixty-odd years ago at seven shillings a week, partly paid in kind. It is a fantastic epitome of the wage madness that has been besetting the world.

One of his cheeks was furrowed by a deep scar, an honourable wound from a somewhat strange action that made history in the village forty years since. On an outlying road had stood an ancient pest-house, which, during an outbreak of smallpox in a town six miles away, the urban authorities had decided to appropriate for the severer cases. Indignation in Thesiger's village at once rose to determined fury. The first van was met by the inhabitants, the horses turned on the road, and the driver threatened into retreat. One of the patients died on the return journey. Open war followed, and the van came back with a strong police escort. Thesiger led his fellows, indignation now in full cry, to the pest-house, and in a few minutes the building was in flames. The charred ruins are still there. The police saw that no more was to be done, but in a scuffle before they left, Thesiger took the mark of a truncheon on

THE FOGGER, PITCHER, LOADER AND RAKERS

his cheek for life. And he and four others helped to make the reputation of a defending counsel, since famous in legal history, at the next Gloucester assizes.

Thesiger had a turn for reading. His was a mixed fare of out-of-date history books and the wilder kind of romance. Out of his learning he had developed a curious but rather proud little self-deception. He told me he was descended from Oliver Cromwell. He offered no explanation of his dignity, merely asserting it. But tactful enquiries in the village did not result in any support for his claim. Indeed, it appeared that it was the effect rather of a general affinity for the great of name than of any particular kinship. It seemed that at times he would transfer his ancestral honours to the Duke of Marlborough, sometimes to Wat Tyler, and on one uproarious occasion at the Chippendale Arms he had been heard to declare with circumstantial fervor that he was in the direct line of descent from Robinson Crusoe.

Somewhere back in his family history, a century and more ago, had been a tragedy. There had been a case of sheep-stealing, a broken-hearted daughter, a betrayal, and a drowning. I fancy to myself that it was Nan Hardwick, Mr Masefield's Nan. Thesiger reckons that those were callous times anyway; you had to be built of hard stuff then. For himself, he earned a pound a week until he stopped regular work. Now he is seventy-seven, and tomorrow morning he will walk across to the far village to draw his weekly old-age pension, ten shillings. Time for I to take a rest, indeed. But he looks good for his hundred and two yet.

John Drinkwater

THE HAYMAKERS

'Ther', ther', ther'. Pat it down. Pat it down. A little more on the fer far corner. Put on a thunderin' good load but don' strain the 'osses. We be in for a wet un to-morra, as sure as thy name's Jack Robbutt.'

'Aa, zur. The owl' zun bin a-zuckin' an't up all th' aat'noon awver Castle Yetton yander.'

'An' the cows be moonin' about, an' the martins be clawss to the ground, an' tha's a sure zign o'

PARK FARM, BLOCKLEY

casulty weather, as my owl' faather used to zaay.'

'As, an' the dews's a-vallin', an' this say 'll soon be as wet as muck, an' the rick's a-yettin now, an' us shan't a done bi doomsday if ya don't look sprack. Go farrud, bwoy, an' pull towwerd a bit. Coom e! Gip now!'

'Lar! dwunt chaestise the poor craturs, maester. The litt!e mer's a-tired. Abin in the shafes all day, ver' nigh.'

There were six toilers engaged with the wagon gathering up the hay. First there were the two pitchers – always considered the principal men of the field; next was the loader; then the two rakers, Jin, the fogger's wife, and Aaron, the odd man, and, last, the youngster to lead the horses, and feed them with handfuls of sweet hay from the wake. A small elm bough, cut from the tree, was hung over the mare's forehead, a half veiling her eyes, to protect her from the troublesome insects. In the middle of the field, beside a haycock, was a large wooden bottle containing the ale, with a tin cup turned upside down over the handle of a spare fork thrust into the earth to render its whereabouts visible.

'Hello! un. Hast thee found thy tongue? Wher's thy man got to today?'

'A yent very well, zur.'

'Aw! Wha's the matter wi' he, then?'

'Got a naesty cowld on 'in.'

'Ev a bin to the chimist?'

'Ae! A went to Hyvuth tha smarnin', awhever. Tha telled un a'd got the – I caen't tell 'e what tha zed.'

'What is it?'

'I caen't tell 'e. You'd oni laaf at ma if e was to't.'

'Come on. Out wi't.'

'I caen't zaay't.'

'Yes, tha cast.'

'Tha telled un a'd got the inifi-zummat.'

'The what?'

'The infliwinzy cowld. Yellacks! I zed you'd oni laugh at ma.'

FAIRFORD

'What! 'Ev a bin sleepin' out under the aay-cocks agyen? Thee must kip un a-twhum o' nights, Jin.'

'Lar! Chent no use to tell 'e nothin'. A takes no moore notice o' I than a crow do o' Zunday.'

'Tell tha what, Jin. Go down to the kitchen, an' missus ull gi' tha a bif bwun. Bile 'e up wi' some suety dumplins. That'll cure 'is cow as sure as God made little apples!'

'Sartintly, zur, an' thenk 'e. Tha's what I'll do, when us a done.'

AARON AND DANIEL

Old Aaron and Daniel, the haymakers, are sceptical when mention is made of prehistoric times. For the physical features of the earth and the fossil remains discovered in the quarries, and ofttimes built into the walls of their houses, they hold Noah's Flood responsible. They believe that stones and minerals grow, and affirm that the sarsens in the meadow get visibly bigger year by year: some of them, they say, are as large again as when they were boys. They are, moreover, positive that bones grow when they are buried in the earth, and that the skeleton of a man or animal will ultimately be enlarged to very much more than its original size. They consider that the prehistoric camp at Blunsdon was made by Oliver Cromwell. The first hunters, according to their idea, were Robin Hood and his merry men. The earliest battles fought were those between King Alfred and the Danes; and they believe that man sprang direct from the Biblical Adam – there can be no doubt whatever about all these things.

But neither Daniel nor Aaron is given to deep and speculative thinking. They love, most of all, during haymaking, and at dinner-time, sitting beneath the thick hedge, fragrant with blossom, or around the trunk of the shady elm or willow beside the sunny river, to talk about past toils and conquests in the field, or divers experiences here and there. Daniel's chief diversion is to tell of the suspicious old farmer who always took a loaded gun to bed with him; the Inglesham Ghost, that appeared in the shape of a black dog; or old Bet Hyde, the witch of Cold Harbour; while Aaron's

NEAR TETBURY

forte is the unromantic tale of John and Sally, first
told by the local roadmender.

John worked on the road for many years, and
Sally was his wife. By and by John got old and tired
of his work. John said to Sally:

'Zally, I thinks I shall gie me job up.'

'Well, if 'e caan't get on wi't, a know, John, gie
't out,' Sally said.

John said: 'I'll gie mi nowtice in to-marra.'

'Aa, zo do,' said Sally.

In the morning John went to master. 'I must jack
it up, maester. I caan't manage it no longer.'

'Well, if you caan't manage it, John, you must gie
't out,' said master.

John went home to Sally. 'I chocked it up, you!'
exclaimed he.

'Aw right, Jacky. We shall get on zum'ow, mun.'

The next day John walked about and seemed
very miserable.

Sally said to John: 'Whyever dossent make thizelf
contented?'

'I caan't, you! I must get another job.'

'What should 'e like to do, then, John?'

'Thinks 'e should like to go to school agyen.'

Sally said, 'I'll go an' zee schoolmaester about it.'

THE MILLER CALLS

THE MOWER

MANGOLD SHREDDING

This she did, and said to him: 'My owl' chap wants to come to school agyen, you!'

'All right,' said the schoolmaster. 'Tell John he can come; we'll see what we can do for him.'

Accordingly John went to school. When he came home at night Sally said:

"Ow dist get on at school?'

'Didn't get on at all, you.'

'Ow's that, then?'

'All the bwoys pinted at ma, an' called ma girt 'ed, an' thick 'ed. Byen a gwain ther' na moore.'

The next day John was as miserable as before. 'Zally,' said he, 'I ull go an' ax gaffer to let ma go back to mi job agyen.'

'Well, zo do, if tha cassent make thizelf contented,' replied Sally.

Then John went to the master and told him about it.

'Yes, John,' said he, 'you can go to your work again.'

John went back with the shovel. Passing along he saw something lying on the road. When he came to it he found it was a small leather bag. John said to himself: 'This'll do aw right vor Zally,' and took the bag home.

'Now, Zally, I got zummat var tha. This'll do djawwsid [deucid] well to kip thi candles in. Durzay thee cast awpen in, Zally, but I caan't.'

After dinner Sally opened the bag, but did not tell John what it contained. It was full of money and notes.

The next day John was out on the road again when a traveller came by. 'Old man, how long have you worked on the road?' said he.

'Aw, zum time, you,' John replied.

'Did you find a bag?'

'Aa-a!'

'Where is it?'

'Too-am. I gied un to Zally to kip 'er candles in.' 'Could I go home and have a look at it?' 'Aa-a! smine t'oot.' They went home together. 'Zally, this vella wants to zee the bag what I vound.' Sally produced the bag.

'Looks very much like my bag. How long have you worked on the road, old man?'

'Aw, gwain in vifty year an' more.'

'And when did you find the bag?'

'The vust day I started to work on the rawd.'

'Well, that can't be mine, then,' said the traveller, and took his departure.

'Aa! but 'twas the zecond time as I worked on the rawd, Zally, ye zee,' John said afterwards.

Alfred Williams

LUKE

''Tis like this – we farm hands be skilled hands, though other folks doesn't seem to reckon as 'tis so. And it be just here as they as comes along finds as there be more to be learnt than 'em thought for. They don't like it neither; it be too rough for 'em, and by rights they've no business here at all. But they wants the same higher wages, all the same, and wet or dry, as the sayin' is, and as though 'em knew'd all about it and was fit to do piecework and make their overtime.'

'They says as livin's dearer. And so it be, some ways. And they says again as there bain't the piecework or variety as was to be had in times gone by. Wull, there's plenty o' tools gone out o' use in my time, and there be a sight more machinery and not the labour wanted as ther' was. And that's true again. But I says this – if a man do like to learn the things as a farmer can never do without, never, and leave the leaden socks at home as he've sometimes got in his shoes, there's as good money to be won on the land as anywheres, and a deal healthier life to be gotten at the same time.'

'I know right enough, as with some as muddles on out here, though the fixed wage, apart from earnings, be a quarter again as high as it wer' as they be worse off now than us was then. When mi father wer' livin' us had a tidy-sized garden and a good piggery, and a good house at eighteenpence. And us had two pigs: killed one, and he helped to pay the rent; brought t'other in house, and rubbed the salt in un of evenings, famous; and with that, and a bit earned harvestin' and piecework, us often did uncommons nicely.'

'And I'll tell yer another thing – there weren't half the sickness them days as there be now. What us did eat wer' good: the bread wer' home made, every crust on it; and the bacon home cured; and so we knew'd what was in the lot, like, and what we was a-puttin' inside. We didn't want so much, neither; nor look for so much, them days. Why, many's the time I've come home with a packet o' rushlights and an ounce o' tea; and that had to last a week' – and Luke laughed loudly at the thought; 'but we was happier then than some ever will let 'emselves he now, for us wer' content, and ther' weren't so much pride and gaddin' and the rest as ther' be these days.'

'My grandfather ever talk of the hungry 'forties, you asks? Ah – times; and what's more, mi father done the same. And they did allus say this – "We did live and wer' merry, and so ment you be. Don't you be upstart: if you be offered a job, no matter what it be – take and do it." Grandfather did only laugh, bless yer, when he spoke o' them times, and 'ould allus finish, same as this – "Us did live – what more did ye want?" They bain't like that now – leastways, not a lot bain't.'

'Ah,' he continued after a pause, 'they old folk – God bless 'em! Kep' on at it all their time, they did; and you may take this as Bible truth, you may – work wer' bred in 'em, I tell yer, and wi' folks o' their metal, it wer' a great denial to 'em when they was forced to give over and felt as they was falterin'.'

There was silence after that. Luke whetted his scythe with the stone he carried at his back in a

WOODCHESTER

belt, and then went to work with a six-foot swing at the tall, rank grass close at hand.

Major Gambier-Parry

THE FAT OF THE LAND

The farmers have the best of everything – beef, mutton, pork, lamb and veal, game and fish, whatever is in season, though here and there you find one that is 'skinny' and 'near', intent on making a pile at the expense of his stomach and appetite. Farmer B—'s choice came out at a gathering over which the vicar presided. Happening to discuss the price of foodstuffs, and of bacon in particular, he amused everyone by declaring his preference for 'that long thin, straked stuff – well, you knows, sir, the be-elly piece!' It is a point to be noticed that those farmers who are strong and hearty in health, fond of a bite and a sup, and whose cellars are well stocked with cider and ale, are always the best natured. Teetotal farmers are usually parsimonious and near, ready to extract the last ounce of labour from the individual; anyone will tell you that in the villages. 'They teetoal vawk bent no good to nobody,' they say.

The village parson usually comes in for a great

STROUD

BURFORD

amount of criticism, though chiefly from outsiders; the villagers themselves are not so unkindly disposed toward him, or the squire either, though they are particularly careful not to place themselves in subjection to them. If there is anything the matter – sickness, accident, or any other misfortune – he is very useful then; he is always willing to do, give, or lend, to each and everyone alike. In bygone years the local doctor used to accept payment in kind from the farmers and villagers – corn from the first, and bacon from the others. This practice is common in some parts today, I am told.

Alfred Williams

REMINISCENCES FROM WITNEY

The services of the band were always at the command of the town for all popular festivals free of charge. The conclusion of peace after the Crimean War afforded an opportunity such as is seldom witnessed in this, or any other town of similar means, at which the band especially distinguished itself. On this occasion a committee was formed of a greater part of the tradesmen of the town, for the purpose of giving vent to the joyous emotions in our hearts. A meeting was called at the Town Hall to ascertain the desires of the principal inhabitants, and to decide in what way it should be commemorated. It was proposed by Mr J. Clinch, banker, that a committee of the whole meeting be formed, and that each one should subscribe two guineas. This was acceded to with two exceptions only.

It was then decided that the whole of the poor of the town should be treated with a dinner on Church Green, of roast beef, plum pudding and beer. The band had contemplated something of the sort, and I was prepared to offer their services gratis, which was readily accepted. The desirability of a treat for all the children, who felt disposed to take part in it, was then discussed, which led to dissent and caused all the fun of the orange in May and the three penny bun. However it was ultimately arranged that the whole of the children of the various schools, the Union children and any other who might appear on Woodgreen, should form a procession with flags and banners supplied from London for the occasion.

COTTAGES AT EBRINGTON

In the meantime sub-committees were formed to canvas the town for help, which was readily responded to. A contract was entered into with Mr J. Gillitt of the Marlboro' Arms Inn to supply the dinner, and the ale was supplied from the brewery of Messrs J.M. Clinch & Co. Tents were erected encircling the greater part of Church Green, with an orchestra for the band at the top.

The morning of the festival, the whole town was in motion and almost every house decorated with devices, motto's flags or evergreens. Several of the latter stretched across the street from house to house and the whole made a very imposing scene.

The children mustered on Woodgreen at midday, about seven hundred in number, and the schools formed respectively, with the Union children in front. Each committee man was provided with a sash and favour made up of red, white and blue, and preceded the band and took the lead of the procession, which was formed in circles on Woodgreen. If I was rightly informed, the first part of the procession reached Church Green before the latter part left Woodgreen, about a mile in length. The children were now regaled with an orange and three penny bun, and dismissed. The tables were then spread with the good things of this life, and each committee man with many others took their station as carvers, supported by all the young, assistants, clerks, shop men etc. etc. as waiters, the band playing a choice selecion of music during dinner.

William Smith

STEAM POWER AT HAILEY

THE SEASON OF MIGRATION

'You can allus tell wh'er a man's a good master er nat bi 'ow 'is work-vawk stops wi'n er le-affs un,' says old Shadrach, who lives in a roomy cottage at the far end of the village. Though this may be accepted as a general axiom, there are exceptions to the rule. Many farm labourers have a natural inclination to rove from place to place, and cannot be cured of the propensity. The old system of fairs encouraged this tendency; the habit of going to be hired became ingrained in the men and youths. As the time came round they began to grow restless, as do birds at the season of migration; they were bound to obey the innate prompting and look about for new quarters.

An almost infallible plan of getting to know whether the men intended to stop at the farm or not was carefully to watch their gardens. If they were kept clean and well-stocked with cabbages and winter greens the farmer was persuaded that Bob or Jack intended to stay with him; but if none of these were planted and the plots were allowed to become untidy, that was a sure sign that the men would be on the move at Michaelmas.

Very often, too, the men would stop at a place but their wives will not consent to it; they have the same inclination as the husbands to change their quarters and experience 'fresh fields and pastures new'. One day, a little before dinner-time, a cowman came to the kitchen door and asked to see master.

'Can I 'ev 'aaf a day off, maaster?' enquired he.

'Oh aa! Thee cast 'ev 'aaf a day, Bob, if thas wants one. Anything the matter?' said the farmer, guessing his intentions.

'No! Don' know as 'tis, maaster.'

'Anything I can do for tha?'

'Nat as I knows on.'

'Anything wrong wi' thi mates, or the cows? Dost want more money, or what is it? Bist dissatisfied at all?'

'No! Nat I byent, but the missis is. A dwun' like the 'owse,' he admitted hesitatingly.

STOW-ON-THE-WOLD LOWER WELL

'Dwun' like the 'owse? But 'tis a good 'owse.'

'The rooms be too big hi 'aaf. 'Er dwun' like un.'

'Well! I tell tha what I'll do. I'll come over an' 'ev a look round, and put some pertitions up an' make the missis comfortable, an' gie tha another shillin' a wik an' ten shillin's extra at Michaelmas. Think it over an' see 'ow tha's like that.'

Thereupon Bob went away, apparently satisfied, and for a week said nothing more about leaving. Then he came to master again and told him it was no good, he did not feel settled, he thought he should go to the fair and get another place. The story of his wife's dissatisfaction with the cottage was invention. The roving fit was upon him; he could not resist the impulse to leave and find a new master.

THE HERDSMAN

The herdsman's cottage stands at the bottom of the street, close beside the tiny inn. Its dull grey walls and roof of thatch, blackened with age, give it a dingy appearance from the outside, but the interior is bright and cheerful, thanks to the good-wife's cleanliness and care, and her desire to have the 'old man' comfortable. There are four fair-sized rooms – two upstairs and two down – to the cottage. The furniture and ornaments are above the average for a labourer to possess, and the whole go to make up an interesting lot, though nothing is held in higher esteem than a certificate for rick building, formerly gained in the local competition. As soon as the herdsman reached home with this he took it to show 'mississ' and 'our young miss', and she declared it must have a suitable frame and paid for one out of her own pocket. A fitch of bacon, wrapped in a newspaper, hangs on one side of the great old-fashioned chimney mellowing in the heat of the wood fire that smoulders beneath.

Many curious odds and ends are poked away in the sideboard and in the old oak drawers – quaint ornaments, photographs, and other things treasured for memory's sake, and last, the cottage stock of medicines, everything prepared of the mandrake, or bryony root, and purchased at the very last cattle show, at which the dealer – a specialist in uses of the root – has a stall every year. Here are boxes of

CHEDWORTH ROMAN VILLA

pills and ointment, embrocation to be rubbed in for sprains, rheumatism, and stiffness, tonics for indi-gestion, a bottle of smelling 'salts', and powders for headache and toothache, warranted to cure in a moment.

'Ther' yent no headache stuff ther', is it?' enquires the good-wife, looking up from her newspaper, that she is reading by the aid of two candles.

'Yes 'tis, fer 'edache an' all an't,' the herdsman replies, rummaging amongst the papers in the drawer.

'Oh Lar'! I wish I'd a know'd that this marnin', then, for I was purty nigh crazy wi't,' says she.

'Then thee oostn't a tuk it,' the cowman answers while the mistress smiles benignly and continues reading the newspaper. . .

''Tis instinct as doos it wi' tha beyassten, else 'ow 'ood thaay know?' says the herdsman, discussing the characteristics of the animals under his charge in the stalls. 'Ther's thaay caavesl I can gie thaay the vly in the middle o' winter wi'ous ever souchin' an 'em.'

'Gie 'em the vly in the winter? Never yerd tell o' that afoore,' says Shadrach.

'Tha's yezzi enuff,' answers she herdsman. 'I goes out in the paddick an' carrs 'em a bit o' 'aay in one 'and. When I gets to 'em, I jest begins buzzin' like a beg vly—"Z-z-z-z-z", an' drives 'em silly. As I ses, is muss be instinct, cos we all knows as there's no vlies about in the winter.'

One day the herdsman is sent for in a great hurry so go down to a neighbouring farm, where a strange accident has happened. A milking cow, in trying to leap a gate, has got half-way over and is hung on the top spar, with all four feet off she ground, and no efforts of the farmer or his men can avail to get her clear of the gate. Bus it is an easy task for the herdsman. He goes to the cow, puts one shoulder under her belly and gives a good grunt and a heave, and she, straining in sympathy with it, leaps over the gate.

One here relates the Cotswold jest of she town youth who had come so learn dairy work. He, being provided with a stool and appointed to milk a nice quiet cow, went into the yard as directed. By and by the farmer at she sop end of the yard heard a scuffling noise and went to see what was the matter. Arrived on the scene he found the youth struggling violently with the beast.

'What b'e got at wi' 'er? Why don' 'e let she cow bide?' said he.

'I can't get the old hussey to sit down, sir,' replied the youth.

HEDGEROW FEASTS

Country children discover a great many edible things in the hedges and fields which are unknown to those who dwell in the towns; they can usually find something or other to munch at all times of the year. In the spring they eat the large buds and young leaves of she hawthorn, commonly known as 'bread and cheese', which are quite palatable; later they devour primrose and cowslip petals and stems, the juicy leaves of the sorrel; afterwards they dig up the underground nuts and eat them, too, and often bite a crowfoot bulb by mistake, which is remarkably hot and pungent. Then in she summer, there is she fruit of the maple tree, 'hatchets and bill-hooks', crabs and wilderns; and in the autumn blackberries, acorns, beech and hazel nuts. 'When these are gone there remain slans (or sloes), peggles (hawthorn fruit), hipsons (the wild-briar berries), and the rich berries of the yew. All these things are gathered and devoured by the youngsters of she countryside, to say nothing of raw wheat and barley, peas and beans, with turnips, swedes, and marigolds from the field.

Alfred Williams

CHEDWORTH VILLA

Winston, Coln Rogers, Coln St Dennis were all built two centuries ago, when the Cotswolds were the centre of much life and activity and the days of agricultural depression were not known. When we look down on their old, grey houses nestling among the great trees which thrive by the banks of the fertilising stream, we cannot hut speculate on their future fate. Gradually the population diminishes, as work gets scarcer and scarcer, 'protection' being granted by law, or the medium of a great European war, or some such far-reaching dispensation of Providence, terrible to think of for those who live to see it, but with all its possibilities of 'good arising out of evil' for future generations, these old villages will contain scarcely a single inhabitant in a hundred years' time. This part of the Cotswold country will once more become a huge open plain, retaining only long rows of tumbled-down stone walls as evidences of its former enclosed state; no longer on Sundays will the notes of the beautiful bells call the toilers to prayer and thanksgiving, and all will be desolation. If only the capitalist or wealthy man of business would take up his abode in these places, all might be well. But, alas! the peace and quiet of such out-of-the-way spots, with all their fascinating contrast to the smoke and din of a manufacturing town, have little attraction for those who are unused to them. And yet there is much happiness and content in these rural villages. The lot of those who are able to get work is a thousand times more supportable than that of the toiling millions in our great cities. There is less drinking and less vice among these villagers than there is in any part of this world that we are acquainted with; consequently you find them cheerful, good-humoured, and, if they only knew it, happy. Grumble they must, or they would not be mortal. Ah! if they could but realise the blessings of the elixir of life – pure air, and fresh, clear, spring water, and sunshine – three inestimable privileges that they enjoy all the year round, and which are denied to so many of the inhabitants of this globe – there would be little grumbling in the Cotswolds.

Let the Cotswold labourer realise that to work on the land, ploughing and reaping, summer and winter, seedtime and harvest, come weal, come woe, is no mean destiny for an honest man; there is scope for the display of a noble and generous spirit in the beautiful green fields as well as in the smoky atmosphere of the east end of London, in a Birmingham factory, or a Warrington forge.

THE RIVER COLN

Coming once more down the hill into the valley of the Coln, we must cross the old Roman road known as the Fosseway, follow the course of the stream, and, about a mile beyond the snug little village of Fossebridge, we reach the great woods of Chedworth.

The extensive Roman remains discovered some years ago in the heart of this forest doubtless formed the country house of some Roman squire. They are well away from the river bank, and about three parts of the way up the sloping hillside. The house faced as nearly as possible south-east. In this point, as in many others, the Romans showed their superiority of intellect over our ancestors of Elizabethan and other days. Nowadays we begin to realise that houses should be built on high ground, and that the aspect that gives most sun in winter is south-east. The old Romans realised this fifteen hundred years ago.

TROUT FISHING

''Tis a most comical job, but the may-fly always comes up thickest of a Sunday,' the keeper frequently exclaims. Then, if you press him for further particulars, he grows eloquent on the subject, and tells you as follows: 'We always reckons to kill the most fish on 'Durby day'. 'Tis a most singular thing, but the 'Durby day' is always the best.'

Now, considering that Derby day is a movable feast, saving that it always comes on a Wednesday, there would appear to be no more logic in this statement than there is in the one about the fly coming up strong on a Sunday. However, so deep rooted is the theory that the Derby and the cream of the may-fly fishing are inseparably associated that we have come to talk of the biggest rise of the season as 'the Derby day', whatever day of the week it may happen to be.

I shall never forget a most lamentable, though somewhat laughable, occurrence which took place live years ago. Foolishly responding to the entreaties of my enthusiastic friend the keeper, I actually did ask five people to fish one 'Durby day'. As luck would have it they all came; but unfortunately a neighbouring squire, who owns part of the water, but who seldom turns up to fish, also chose that day, and with

THE RIVER COLN

him came his son. Seven was bad enough in all conscience, but imagine my feelings when a wagonette drove up, full of undergraduates from Oxford: my brother, who was one of the undergraduates, had brought them down on the chance, and without any warning. Of course they all wanted to fish, though for the most part they were quite innocent of the art of throwing a fly. Result: ten or a dozen fishermen, all in each other's way; every rising fish in the brook frightened out of its wits; and very little sport. The total catch of the day was only thirty trout, or exactly what three rods ought to have caught.

These were the sort of remarks one had to put up with: 'I say, old chap, there's a d—d fellow in a mackintosh suit up stream; he's bagged my water'; or, 'Who is that idiot who has been flogging away all the afternoon in one place? Does he think he's beating carpets, or is he an escaped lunatic from Hanwell?'

The whole thing was too absurd; it was like a fishing competition on the Thames at Twickenham.

Since this never-to-be-forgotten day I have come to the conclusion that to have too few anglers is better than too many; also, alas! that it is quite useless to ask your friends to come unless they are accomplished fishermen. It takes years of practice to learn the art of catching south-country trout in these days, when every fish knows as well as we do the difference between the real fly and the artificial. One might as well ask a lot of schoolboys to a big 'shoot', as issue indiscriminate invitations to fish.

J. Arthur Gibbs   FAIRFORD

ANDOVERSFORD

AROUND THAMES HEAD

Around the source of the Thames is clustered a group of ancient villages and hamlets containing many imposing farmhouses and cottages. Half a mile below its source the spring was forded by a road, and foot passengers crossed on stepping-stones. By daylight the journey was safe, but at night it was attended with risks, especially when the springs were high. Then most people waded and ignored the stones. Will Darby, the short-sighted old tile-digger, found them by instinct and could usually cross in safety, though once, at least, he came to grief. That day he had been to Ciceter Mop and was returning in a state of mental elevation. 'I shall go into the bruk tonight, as sure as the day,' he repeated to himself on the road. When he came to the stones he put the wrong foot forward, missed at the second step, and went floundering into the stream.

The abolition of the local inn has metamorphosed the life of the place, and sports and games have disappeared, though there were many amusements formerly. In addition to the annual festival of Jackiman's Club a village wake was held at which there was morris-dancing for ribbons, back-swording, and wrestling. Agriculture and stone-digging comprised the principal out-of-doors work; wool-spinning was carried on in the cottages. Wassailing was the favourite sport at Christmas-time, and the jovial custom was observed in all the villages upon the banks of the Thames streamlet. The wassailers rigged themselves out in fancy dress and carried a bowl decorated with ribbons and holly round to the farmhouses, where they sang their merry song and received money and ale. The effigy of an ox preceded the company as they journeyed from house to house. The effigy was formed of the skin of an ox set on a skeleton frame, with the head and foreparts stuffed with straw, and with two bottles for eyes. Two sturdy wassailers crept inside and bore it along, imitating the motions of the beast, to the delight of the rustics.

BLEDINGTON

CRICKLADE STREET, CIRENCESTER

NAILSWORTH

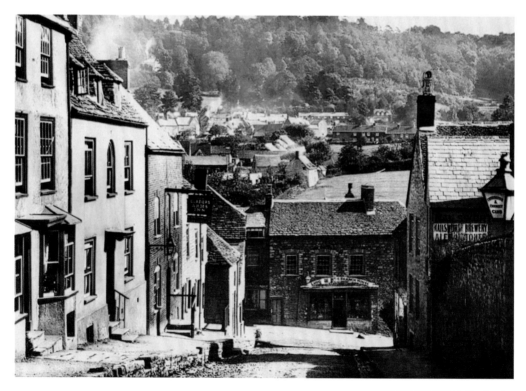

WOTTON-UNDER-EDGE

BURFORD

The last inn at Kemble was kept by one 'Damper' Adams, who was a maker of wooden ploughs. He sold such notoriously bad ale that a gang of men set upon the house, rolled out the casks, smashed in the heads, and sent the beer tumbling down the hill into the river.

Ewen – pronounced 'Yeowin' by the rustics – possesses neither church nor stately mansion, but it has many picturesque farms and cottages and it is backed with magnificent timber. No spot on the Thames is more beautiful, and certainly none is more healthy, to judge from the great age and appetites of its inhabitants. Centenarians are almost as much the rule as the exception, and for hearty appetite who could excel the redoubtable Cornelius Uzzle that, in the presence of living witnesses, unostentatiously devoured twelve pounds of bacon – six pounds raw and six pounds parboiled – at one meal for a wager at the old Wild Duck Inn? The thatched cottage by the roadside yonder has had but two tenants in a hundred and fifty years. The aged occupant's memory extends back through his father for nearly two centuries.

Alfred Williams

CAPS OF QUALITY

To go shopping in a place like Burford is not at all necessarily to get what you want, certainly not to get it with swiftness; but it is to negotiate with persons of dignity and ruminating character – persons of resource too. Behind our ironmonger's unpretending frontage lurks a most efficient working array of machine tools; we buy drugs at our chemist's to an organ accompaniment; the Burford post master is motor proprietor, chauffeur, and photographer. And it is not the men alone who possess dignity and character. One elderly tradesman tells a tale that delights me in connection with an oil portrait of his grandmother that hangs on his wall. She is wearing a monumental cap decorated with artificial fruits and flowers, and by this hangs the story. A good manager, she had never been troubled by her husband for details of household or personal expenditure. He had accepted her caps as a matter of course,

COLLEGE YARD TENANTS, BURFORD

until one day he came by accident on the bill, of a guinea, for this one. Thereupon he fell into a rage, declaring that no such extravagance should be allowed in a house where he was master. Very well, his wife replied, but if she could not wear the quality of caps that befitted her, she would not wear any. And to this resolution she held for the remainder of her life, in spite of all her husband's solicitations to the contrary. 'And so,' her grandson comments in telling the story, 'I learned to let well alone; especially where a woman comes into the question.'

THE CRAFTSMAN

Why was it, I found myself asking a group of builder's men working for me in 1928, that only the elders among them could do the dry-walling? Because the younger man was not apprenticed nowadays, I was told. Why not? Because, after the years of apprenticeship, he would earn only one and twopence an hour, and that only intermittently, while the altogether untrained man would be regularly earning his shilling an hour – only twopence an hour more, even when at a job, for all those years of waiting and for skill.

Henry Bond I had come to know first when I had jammed the lock of my desk, and had sent to ask him to mend it. I came in to find him bending over the desk, a bag of tools beside him. He touched his forelock, as he did always before speaking, and said, his voice falling a note sadly,

'He won't unlock, you locked him all right.' The voice grew eager and then fell again, amusedly. 'Yes, he locked right enough, but he won't unlock. Ye-es.' A bit sadly we stood facing our problem. 'I'll have to take him off.' Again the tone fell a shade.

'Will that be difficult?' I asked.

'No, oh no. I can take him off; well, yes, I can take him *off*,' and the tone rose a note.

I left him at that and went out of doors. Coming back, I stopped beneath my window; the air was filled with a rich, though muted, humming. Cautious as I tried to be, he must have heard my footstep, for I came up the stairs into silence. As I re-entered the room he was carrying the lock to the window, screwing up his large face and cocking his best eye to see what was amiss. Then, with his big hands, he showed me what the key wanted.

WHARF AT EASTINGTON

'He don't catch,' he explained; 'he needs another piece' – the piece indicated was microscopic. The tone now was eager, confident; he was at grips with the difficulty. 'I'll take him away with me,' he said positively. 'You mustn't lock with him, for you'd lock him again,' he chuckled; 'he locks right enough but he don't unlock.' He gathered up his tools.

'And what do I owe you?' I asked.

'We-ell,' he spoke with surprise – the job he saw as important, but the payment! – 'but I ain't made him yet; no, I ain't made him ye-et.'

'I may be out when you bring the key,' I said, 'I would much rather pay you now.'

'Oh, well,' he soothed, conceding to my impatience, 'sixpence would it be perhaps?' naming the sum as if he just hoped it might be permissible. I produced the sixpence and he took it reluctantly, the key not being mended yet, as from one whose impetuosity must be humoured, saying that was kind of me, unnecessarily kind. 'Thankee, ma'am, thank you very kindly.'

Mary Sturge Gretton

THE BARGEMAN

The village of Kempsford is poor in appearance. A single street runs from end to end of the place, and the cottages, many of them little, old, dilapidated buildings, stand ranged in rows and groups, with doors opening on to the road. Half-way down the Street is the village green, and in the centre of this Stands a large elm, called by the inhabitants 'stocks tree', and 'crass tree', because it was there that the ancient market cross and stocks were formerly situated.

The canal, that cuts across from Inglesham to Kempsford, almost touches the river beyond the church and then continues away to Cricklade. There are several locks of great depth between Inglesham and Kempsford, and others occur at intervals to beyond the Thames Head. They bear witness to the constant rise towards the river's source; it is far greater than you would guess by merely following the channel of the stream. The stones that compose the bases of the bridges are ready to tumble into the shallow water; the wharves are ruined, the tow-path deserted, and the bed is choked with vegetation.

SOUTH CERNEY

'The closin' o' this canal was like takin' a link out o' the middle of a chain,' says the old bargeman as he sits and calmly smokes his pipe, while his wife stitches away at a new shirt for her grandson, and looks over the top of her spectacles to note the effect of her good-man's words. For more than half a century they had lived in the barges. Backwards and forwards, year after year, they travelled with their burdens of corn, cheese, coal, stone, and timber, at one time frozen in for weeks at a stretch, at another aground for days in the dark tunnel, and again washed out into the mouth of the Severn by the boisterous tide. Yet, though they had suffered hardships, they were fond of the life and were never so happy as when gliding through the beautiful meadows, or halting for the night in some secluded spot above the lock, where the spouting water gushes out musically of a warm summer's evening. Both the bargeman and his wife are stout and robust. 'It don' look as if it 'urted am an us, do it?'

THE TRIP TO CRICKLADE

'Be 'e gwain to Cricklut, mother?' enquired the barge-man, Adam Twine, of the stout old dame who, with basket on arm, took the tow-path at Marston bridge on her way to the town one afternoon.

'Aa, I be,' she replied.

'If you likes to jump in you can ride. We be off directly,' said he.

'Oh Lar'! I never bin aboord ship but I'll come wi' thee. 'Tool rest mi vit an' legs a bit,' answered the old woman.

Accordingly she got in and went below and sat in the cabin, and the two conversed on various subjects. Meanwhile the boat had started noiselessly and without a tremor. The boy was at the rudder and the conversation was maintained. By and by mother become fidgety.

''Ow much longer bist agwain to be afoore thas starts?' she enquired at length.

'Afoore 'e starts!' exclaimed old Adam.

'Aa! cos I be tired o'waitin' yer. 'E could a got 'aaf-way ther' bi this time,' she continued.

'We shall stop in two or dree minutes, mother,' said the boatman.

'Stop another two or dree minutes! Why essent a telled ma as tha wassent agwain to start afoore, nat kip anybody yer an' make a fool an ma. I could a got ther' bi now if I 'edna looked aater thee,' cried she, burning with indignation.

Just then the boat gave a bump – they had come alongside the wharf.

'Yer us be, mother. You can get out now, an' mind not fall in an' be drownded,' said Adam.

MALMESBURY ROAD, CRICKLADE

'Lark a massey! What! be we at Cricklut, then? An' I didn' know as we'd a started,' exclaimed she, stepping out of the boat in amazement.

Alfred Williams

REMINISCENCES OF EMIGRATION FROM FILKINS

I ploughed and sowed the land, milked the cows, and mother made the cheese – the greatest part of which we sent to London. I had my breakfast beside a cheese tub every summer for twenty six years, but about this time my companion, the cow dealer's son, went to America and I wanted to go with him. My father and mother was terribly afraid I should go and talked me out of it, and another young man agreed to go with him. But on the morning he started his heart failed him, so he had to go by himself and he purchased a small farm over there, and before he had held it a year another man came and claimed it – he had bought it of the wrong owner and so lost all he had, but a gentleman took compassion on him and lent him some money to commence cow dealing again, and he got a wealthy man and returned to see me thirty years after, but looked a deal older than myself although I was several years older.

I had another companion as went to America – a circumstance occurred while he was there, I was walking up the fair at Lechlade when a young girl was a-looking over a garden wall and something seemed to say to me 'if so-and-so was to come back from America and marry that girl,' however he did come back from America and did marry that very girl and went back to America again.

Thomas Banting

EMIGRATION OF PAUPER CHILDREN

Seven workers' children, whose emigration to Canada has recently been the subject of negotiation by Baron de Ferrieres and his co-members of the emigration and boarding-out committee, have started for their new homes. They were seen off at the station by two or three of their guardians. Arrangements were made to have them seen to at Birmingham, and a telegram subsequently was received to the effect that they had arrived in the best possible spirits at Liverpool. On the following morning they were safely placed on the Allan steamer Peruvian, under the care of Miss MacPherson, who was taking out to Toronto a number

GREAT BARRINGTON

of boys from London. The same afternoon, the Peruvian steamed out of dock, but anchored in the Mersey till the stiff gale then blowing should moderate. She has since proceeded towards her destination.

The Gloucester Journal

THE ODD JOB MEN

'Master' Kemble is everybody's man, and the old road-mender's in particular. He does work for everyone in the place almost, but is chiefly at home as a drover. He is the one homeless person of the village. All make use of him, but none own him. He does a job here and a job there; takes cattle to market and sells them, and brings back the cash; deals in faggots and firewood, sticking wood for peas and clothes-props, watercresses and mushrooms – anything to get an honest copper. He is very rough in appearance, as drovers often are; yet he is a farmer's son. His father got into low water, and when the old people died, several of the boys fell away, and would not be bound to a master. This is common in the agricultural fraternity: they are proud in misfortune, and will not forget their former circumstances: they will often remain bare and destitute rather than cringe to another. Whether such a course is compatible with wisdom or not – as the world knows it – is questionable. At any rate, it is characteristic, and many will admire it.

Kemble serves all, quarrels with all, and is reconciled with all in turns; for, though poor, he is independent, and will not be put upon. He is frequently told to 'get out of here, and never set foot on my premises any more'; but in a few days he turns up again, and solicits food, or a drink of ale or cider, and is not refused. Perhaps he presents himself at the kitchen door, wet and cold, and half famished, but cheerful as May, and begs for his breakfast; no matter what the offence has been, the farmer takes compassion on him, and serves the meal. For dinner he visits someone else, and another for supper, or he may share the road-mender's hospitality, and afterwards help him with his garden. His bedroom is chiefly the open air, his canopy the heavens, his candle the stars. He is often warned as to the perils of the course of life he leads, but he laughs at all advice, however sincerely proffered. 'I be all right, naybur,

LOWER SLAUGHTER

dun you fret. Lode bless tha, I be as 'appy as all the
birds in the ayr.'

Ryder was a castaway, an odd man of the village;
a poor, simple fellow, as harmless as a lamb to all
but himself, whose failing was merely a fondness
for a glass of beer. His old father was shepherd at
Rove's Farm; he had brothers and sisters well-to-
do. When they shifted he could not be torn from
the locality; he had a real love for the old scenes
and faces. Part of the year he spent in training
with the county militia; at other periods he went
haymaking and harvesting, and doing odd work.
It is even useful to have such a man about the
village; he is sure to be wanted from time to time.
As to his military career, he came to be sergeant
there. In the hay or harvest field he was always
'shoulder arms', 'right about face', and so on, and
wanted to drill every youth he came in contact
with. He slept under the haystack, or among the
sheaves, or in a shed somewhere or other. But
when the years crept upon him he found the life
beset with hardships; poor, destitute, failing in
health, and outcast, no one wanted Ryder any
more. One morning – there had been a sharp

HIS CANOPY THE HEAVENS

GREAT RISSINGTON

frost – he was found on the towpath under the hedge, dead; his face was upturned, his clothes were frozen stiff. He had not been well, but was seen about the night before. It was thought he was faint with weakness, and fell into the water, but got out and dragged himself under the hedge, and died from exposure. Perhaps no one mourned for him, but that is the fate of many poor.

Bill Brittin was as hard as flints. He lived in Pigeon House Cottage, and had relatives in London, whom he sometimes visited. When he went there he wore a corduroy suit, coloured kerchief round the neck, billy-cock hat, and heavy boots, with a ground-ash stick in his hand. He carried a turnip watch, with silver chain dangling down. A good many of the cockneys stared hard at him, nodded and smiled, and many addressed him, very often to their sorrow. 'Morning, John,' this one said. 'Is that you, John?' 'Come again, John?' 'How do you do, John?' and so on. This one hailed him as an old companion, another tried to show him something; many dodges were tried to befool the old rustic, but not for Brittin. 'You 'old on, mate,' 'No you dwunt, mate,' 'No thenk ee, mate,' he replied to everything; and often his answers were too forcible to be repeated. 'Does your watch go, John?' this one enquires. 'Go? aa coorse a do, ya vool! goes when I carrs un,' Brittin replies; he was not to be caught napping. His favourite stopping-place was

GYPSY PEGLER

LOWER GUITING

the Load of Hay, at Paddington. 'A pint o' ale and a pennoth o' bren cheese,' was his fare, 'and ther went dripence.' He was one of the old type.

Alfred Williams

THE SHADOW O' BIZLEY STEEPLE

'Willum,' said I, as I met my old friend this week, 'I have come to the conclusion that you do not appreciate half enough the wonderful beauties of your district. Why, in some places I know of the inhabitants spend thousands in advertising the attractions of their neighbourhood, when such attractions cannot be compared with the natural beauties which are showered upon you in this part of Gloucestershire.'

The sun was shining in a cloudless sky; a keen invigorating wind was blowing across the valley, larks were carolling joyfully as they rose higher and higher towards the azure heavens. I had felt something like Shelley must have felt when he burst into that glorious hymn 'To a Skylark':

Hail to thee, blythe spirit!
Bird thou never wert.

It seemed to me that heaven and earth, things seen and unseen, birds and all cattle, mountains and all hills, all the green things upon the earth, were

LOWER SLAUGHTER

THE SEVERN VALE FROM RODBOROUGH

joining in one harmonious chorus and singing 'Bless ye the Lord, praise Him and magnify him for ever.'

'Yuss, tis vurry bu'ful,' remarked Willum, 'but Jar' bless 'ee, yoke about hyur dwunt thank much o' thuk zart o' theng. Davy Buship, f 'r instans, 'ood ice more beauty astanding scratting the back o' one o' 'ees pegs an' sniffing on um than he 'ood if you wuz to putt un avoor yander 'ood an' tell 'n as he wuz to hadmire the beauties o' Nachur. You ice, these yur thengs as you do thenk zo much on we 'ave zid ever zence we wuz childurn; we knaws as the valley down below 'ool kum up smiling every spreng time, an' thur dwunt zeem anytheng to go into sturrix auver, acause tis bound to happen where or no. An' tis only them thengs as you byent used to zeeing as maakes you shout wi' raptyur. Not, mind you,' – the old fellow continued deprecatingly – 'as I meself dwunt like to zee the 'oods like they be now, acause I do.'

'But, Willum, just look at this beautiful landscape,' I cried, pausing in the road and looking across the valley where the Severn lay like a huge diamond sparkling in the sunlight.

'Oh! ah! tis bu'ful, thur's no zaying as went,' agreed Willum, 'maake I thenk o' that as we be tawld on in Revulations. I often thanks as Heaven wunt be Heaven unless thurs green trees and blue skies, an' zenging birds. I knaws 'tis auld-vashjoned to talk o' Heaven as zif twuz a plaace whur the birds do zeng an' evrytheng i bu'ful. But our Saviour talked on 't like that an' called it Paradise, an' thur wuz all them bu'ful thengs in Paradise, a clear viowing river, an' vine green trees. An' He's the only one as rally knaws, zo I vur one blieves wot He do zay. Thurs a place up Zizziter woy in Lard Bathurst's 'oods as they do call Paradise, an' well they might, vur us one o' the prettiest spots in all the park. 'Ave you ever been theta?'

'No,' I said, 'but I hope to go.'

As we walked on Willum pointed out several things to me which had escaped my notice before.

'Doost zee thuk thur Church Spire?' said he, pointing right across the hills.

After some searching I discovered it.

'Well, tha's Bizley Steeple; evur been to Bizley?'

'Yes, I drove through it once – a very old-world place.'

'You med well zay thuk,' replied Willum – 'why it do zumtimes go by the nyem of "Bizley-God-help-

STROUD ROAD, BISLEY

us". I can't azactly tell 'ee why, but I have yeerd it
zed as twuz acause long ago they used to be cut off
vrom everybody in the winter and thengs 'ood get
pretty bad wi' urn. But 'tis a nisish place nowadays.
Thuk thur steeple you can zee vur miles an' miles
round, an' they do tell I as vur dree marnins in the ur,
that is the day acvoor the zhartest day, the zhartest
day, an' the day after, you can zee the shadow o'
Bizley Steeple on Ham'ton Common if you do get
up early enough.'

'But surely Minchinhampton Common is many
miles away,' I said.

'Well, tha's wot they do zay, I a'nt a gone up to
zee vur meseif, but p'raps, now, you cood just vind
out vur yurself in the zummer.'

'Perhaps so,' I said. But I have my doubts, for I
share with Dr Arnold and many lesser characters a
reluctance to leave my bed in the morning.

'Now, doost zee that Valley?' continued the old
man, as he pointed in another direction. 'Tha's
Cha'ford Valley, or as zum do call't the Golden
Valley. I an' bin much o' a gadabout meself, but if
thur's a prittyr place wi'in vifty mile I a'nt zid it nor
yeerd ons. Jus' luk at them thur 'oods. Zee 'ow the
beech trees be one shade o' green an' the larch trees
tan' just now I should thenk as every shade can be
vound on the slopes o' Cha'ford Valley. If you a' got
any vrends akumming down you myek um spend a

FAR OAKRIDGE

BISLEY

vyow coppers an' go be motor to Cha'ford. They
cood get up thur and then along the top so Ham-
ton Common 'bout 'leven in the marnin' and tyek
a bot o' gub wi' im. Let um walk up Cowkum Hill
whur they cood yet their bit o' tommy and then
spend the aternoon on the Common, an' get down
to Brimskum avoor dark.'

'I will certainly suggest it to my friends I see,' I
remarked.

'Then another day,' Willum went on, 'they cood
go to Cha'ford agyen, an' walk up tuther side o'
the valley round by Cha'ford Church, up drew
the Vrith 'ood as is alukking vurry vine just now.
Zum o' our young yoke told I as they cood spend
a whole day in thuk 'ood an' not get tired. Then
you can walk auver to Bussige, an' although I zes it
as shouldn't, if thus wun prittyur view nor another
about here tis the one vrom Bussige Churchyard.
Then you cood walk down the valley and back
agyen to Brimskum.'

We had reached Willum's home. I bade him
'Good-night' and walked down she valley fully
persuaded to try the walks the old fellow had
suggested to me.

C. Edmund Hall   TUNLEY

Glossary

The following words are by no means all that are used in the Cotswold dialect; a full listing would require a dictionary of its own. Because of the phonetical nature of dialect there is not necessarily any proper method of spelling, and the following represent the main 'sound'.

A-GWINE A-going, going
AGWAIN A-going, going
ATER After
ABIDE To endure
ADRY Thirsty
AFEARED Frightened
AFORE Before
AGEN Opposite to, against
ANNEAL To shape by softening
ANNEARST Near
ANUNST Over against
ARTISHREW The shrew
ATHERT Across
ATERMATH Grass after mowing
AYERD Heard
AWAY WITH To bear with
AX, AXE To ask
AXEN Ashes

BACK-SIDE The back of a house
BAD To beat husks
BAG The udder of a cow
BALD-RIB Spare-rib
BANOORE A cello
BAN-NUT The walnut
BARKEN The homestead
BARN Yeast
BARROW-PIG A gelt pig
BASTE To beat
BAT-FOWLING Netting birds at night
BAULK A bank or ridge
BEASTS Horned cattle
BEHOLDEN Indebted to
BELLY To swell out
BELLUCK Bellow
BENNET, BENT Dry standing grass
BESOM A word of reproach
BETEEM To indulge with
BIDE To stay, to dwell
BIN Because
BISN'T Be you not, are you not
BITTLE Beetle, a heavy mallet
BLATHER To talk indistinctly
BLIND-WORM Slow-worm
BLOWTHE Blossom
BODY An individual
BOOT Help, defence
BOTTOM A valley
BRAKE A small coppice
BRASH Light stony soil
BRAVE Healthy
BRAY Hay, spread to dry
BRIT SHED Over-ripe corn
BRIZZ The gad-fly
BROOK To endure
BROW The abrupt ridge of a hill
BUCKING Dirty linen

BUDOE To move a short distance
BUFF To stammer
BURDEN As much hay or straw as a man can carry
BURR Calf sweetbread
BURROW Any shelter
BUTRY A comrade in labour

CADDLE To busy with trifles
CANDER Yonder
CANOEK-LUCKS Look yonder
CANDLE-MASS BELLS Snowdrops
CANDLE-TINNINO Candle-lighting
CANT To toss lightly
CARK Care
CASALTY, CASULTY Casualty, in context of 'failing to be right'
CASN'T, COUSSENT Can't, Can you not
CHAM To chew
CHAR A job (charwoman)
CHARM A noise, clamour
CHATS The chips of wood when a tree is felled
CHAUDRON Entrails of a calf
CHAW To chew
CHAWN To gape
CHILVEK A ewe-lamb
CHISSOM To bud forth
CHITLINOA Chitterlings, pig's small intestine
CHOCK-FULL Full to choking
CHURK The udder of a row
CLAMMY Sticky
CLAVEY Chimney-piece
CLEATS A small wedge
CLEAVE To burst hard bodies asunder
CLOUT A heavy blow
COLLY The blackbird
COLT A landslip
COMB A valley with only one inset
COMICAL Strange
COO-TER The wood pigeon's note
COUNT To consider, to suppose
CRAB A stick from a crab-apple tree
CRANK A dead branch of a tree
CRINCH A morsel

DAAK To dig up weeds
DADDLES Said, playfully, of the hands
DADDOCKY Said of decayed timber
DAP To sink and rebound
DAP-CHICK A bird, the little grebe
DARZE Damn
DAY-WOMAN A Dairymaid
DEADLY A word meaning intenseness in a bad sense, as 'deadly stupid'
DESIOHT A blemish
DESFERD Beyond measure, extremely
DISANNUL To annul
DISMAL An evil in excess

DISSENT, OIS'NT Didn't you
DO'EE, DO YOU Will you, 'Do 'ee please come', 'will you please come'
DOFF To take off clothing
DOLLOP A lump, a mass of anything
DON To clothe, to put on
DOUT To extinguish a light
DRAT, DRATTED Expression of vexation
DRINK Used as a term for beer
DROXY Decayed wood
DRUNGE To embarrass
DUDDLE To stun with noise
DUDGEON Ill temper
DULKIN, DELKIN A small dell or dale
DUMMLE Dull, slow, stupid
DUNCH, DUNNY Deaf, an imperfection
DWUN Don't

ELVER A small eel
ENTENNY The main doorway of a house
ER Her, but sometimes used also for he 'he did this', 'er did this'
ETTLES Nettles
EYAS A young hawk
EYE A brood of pheasants

FAGGOT Derogatory term for old woman
FAGGOT Cut wood
FALL Autumn, to grow yellow
FEND To forbid
FILLS Shaft of a can
FILTHY, VILTRY Filth of any kind
FLAKBS A wattled hurdle
FLICK The fat between the bowels of a slaughterrd animal
FLOWSE Flawing, flaunting
FLUMP Applied to a heavy fall
FOGGER An agricultural labourer, usually involved in livestock feeding
FORE-RIGHT Opposite to
FOR-WHY Because
FRITH Young white thorn
FROIRE Frozen
FROM-WARD Opposite to 'toward'
FRUM, FROOM, FREM, FRIM Full, abundant
GAITLE To wander idly
GAITLING An idler
GALLOW To alarm, frighten
GALORE An exclamation of abundance
GAMUT Sport
GEAR Harness, apparel
GIMMALS Hinges
GLOWR To stare moodily
GLOUT To look surly
GLUM, GLUMF Gloomy
GODE Past tense of 'to go'
GRIF A drain
GRIT Sandy, stony land
GROUNDS Fields, grass-lands
GROUTS, GRITS Oatmeal
GULCH A fat glutton
GULLY A deep ravine
GUMPTION Spirit, sense, quirk obaervation
GURGINS The coarse meal of wheat
GURT Great
GYET Gate

HAINE To shut up a meadow for hay
HALE To draw with violence, or a team

HANDY Near, convenient
HANK A skein of any thread
HARBOUR To abide
HARSLET The main entrails of a pig
HASSENT Hadn't
HATCH A door which only half fills the doorway
HAULM Dead stalks
HAUNCHED To be gored by cattle
HAY-SUCK Hedge-sparrow
HAYWARD An officer appointed at the court
HAZBN To chide
HEATHER The top-binding of a hedge
HERR Weight, burden
HELE To cove
HELIAR A thatcher
HIC-WALL The green woodpecker
HIGHST To uplift
HILLARO, HILWARD Towards the hill
HILT see Yelt
HINGE The liver, lungs, and heart of a sheep
HISSEN His
HIVE To cherish
HOG A sheep of either sex, one year old
HOLT A high wood
HOOP The bulfinch
HOPE A hill
HOUSEN Plural of houses
HUT or HOT; Past tense of 'to hit'

INGLE Fondling, favourite
ININ, INNION The onion
INNARDS The intestines

JARL The title 'Earl'
JETTY To thrust out
JIGGER To put out of joint
JOGGET A small load of hay
JOMETRY Geometry, considered almost magic
JOWL The jaw bone
JUNKETS Sweetmeats, dainties

KALLENGE Challenge, as pronounced
KECK To heave at the stomach
KEECH A lump of congealed fat
KEER LUCKS Look here
KERFE A cutting from a hayrick
KINCH The young fry of fish
KITTLE Anything requiring nice management

LAGGER A Long strip of land
LAIKING Idling, playing truant
LAMB To beat
LANDAM To abuse with rancour
LARROP To beat, to flog
LATTERMATH Grass after mowing
LAYTER The full amount of eggs laid by a bird
LEE, LEW Shelter from wind or rain
LEECH A cow doctor
LEER Empty, hungry
LEESE To glean corn
LIBBET A shred, a tatter
LICKER Drink, alchoholic
LIFF, LIEVER Rather more inclined to
LIGHTING STOCK Step for mounting a horse
LIKE A frequent pleonasm, as 'dead-like', 'pretty-like'
LIMBER Weak, pliant, flagging
LIMP Flabby, flexible
LINCH A small precipice, usually grass covered
LINNET Flax dressed, but not twisted to thread

LISSOME Active, nimble
LITHER Light, active, sinewy
LIZZEN A chasm in a rock
LIMBER Weak, pliant, flagging
LOP To cut growing wood
LUG A measure of land, a perch
LUSH Abundant, flourishing
LUSTY Strong, in full health

MAIN Expression of emphasis, 'Main dull', 'awfully dull'
MAKE Mate, companion, lover
MATE Meat
MAUNDER To ramble in mind
MERE A strip of grass as a boundary in open fields
MICHE, MYCHE, MOOCHE To idle, play srusns
MIDDLIN, MIDDLNG Of indeterminate or poor health
MILT The spleen
MIND To remember
MINE Depending on context, husband or wife
'MIRE To wonder, to admire
MIRKSHET Twilight
MOIL, MYLE To labour, so toil
MORING-AXE A pick-axe
MORT A vast quantity
MORTAL Excessively, extremely
MOSSEL Morsel
MOUND A fence, a boundary
MUN An affirmative interjection, probably 'Man'
MUSSIFUL Merciful, mindful
MUST The crushed apples or pears pressed for cider or perry
MYEM Mean, meaning of

NAGGLE, NIGGLE To tease, so fret
NALE An alehouse
NARH A little
NARON None, never, ne'er one
NATION Very
NATRAL Naturally
NEIVE The hand
NESH Weak, tender
NOT, NOTTED Applied so cattle without horns
NUNCHEON Luncheon

ODDS A difference between two specimens or statements
ON Of, 'One on 'em', 'One of them'
OODLE, HOODLE, WOOD-WAH The nightingale
OONT or WOONT The mole
OR Before, 'ere
OETS Chaff, any worthless matter

PACE To raise with a lever
PARGITEE A plasterer
PEASEN Plural of peas
PELT To throw stones, etc.
PICK A hay fork
PIDDLE To trifle
PILL The pool caused by she junction of two streams
PIRGY Quarrelsome
PITCH To fall down heavily
PLASH A small pool
PLEACH To intertwine she branches of pollards for hedging
PLIM To swell with moisture
PLY To bend
POLLARDS A mixed crop of peas and beans
POSSY A great number
POVEY An owl
PRIZE To weigh

PRONG A large hay-fork
PUCK A quantity of sheaves stacked together
PUB The udder of a cow
PURE In good health
PURL To throw with violence

QUAR A stone quarry
QUARREL A square pane of glass
QUICKSET Young whitethorn for hedges
QUIST A woodpigesn
QUITCH Couch-grass
QUOB, QUOP To tremble
QUOMP To subdue

RAG To chide, to abuse
RAMES Dead stalks
RAMSHACKLE To move noisily, in a loose, disjointed manner
RATH Early, quirk, rash
RAUGHT The past tense of reach
RAVES The rails which surround the bed of a wagon
RAVELMENT Entanglement
REED Counsel
REEN A small stream
RETCH To strain before sickness
RIME Hoar-frost
RIVE To split asunder
RONOS Rungs of a ladder
ROVE The past tease of Rive
RUCK A crease in a garment
RUMPLE To discompose linen, bedding, wearing apparel
RUSTY Spoken of rancid bacon

SCORT The hoof-marks of horses, cattle, deer
SCREECH A bird, the swift
SCREECH-DROSSLE The missel-thrush
SCRUB Shrubs
SCRUSE Past tense of squeeze
SEG Stale human urine used in the manufacture of woollen cloth
SHARD A breach in a fenre
SHATTERS Fragments of broken pottery, glass
SHIDE A small plank, a piece of wood
SHOT OF Got rid of
SIGHT A vast number
SLAMMERKIN A slut
SLANS Sloes
SLEIGHTS Downland used solely for pasture
SLICK Slippery
SLINGE Stolen wool from a clothier
SLIVER A slice
SNEAD The handle of a scythe
SNITE To blow the nose
SNOUL A lump, particularly bread, cheese or she like
SPIT A spade
SPRACK Lively, brisk, vigorous
SPREATHE To have the hands or face roughened by frost
SPURTLE To sprinkle with any fluid
STANK A pool caused by a dam on a stream
STRAIGHTWAYS Immediately
SWICH Such

TACK Drink, alcoholic
TALLUT The hayloft
TATERS Potatoes
TED To spread abroad new-mown gross for hay
TEEM To empty; spoken of a tub
TEG A lamb
TESTER Sixpence

THEAVE A ewe in she second year
THIC, THACH This, that
TICE To entice
TICKLE Uncertain in temper
TINE To kindle
TRIG Ness, quick, ready
TUD An apple dumpling
TUMP Earth thrown up
TUSSOCK A thick tuft of gross
TWINK The chaffinch
TWISSLE To turn about rapidly
TWITCH To touch
TYNING An enclosure from a common field
TYUK Take

UNKARD, UNKET Unknown, uncouth, lonely
UPSHOT The amount of reckoning, the outcome

VALUE, VALLY Used with much the some meaning as
Upshot
VENTERSOME Heedless, daring
VOLK Folk, people
VINNEY Mildewed, mouldy
VITTALS Victuals, food
VORRUD Forward
VOSSLE, FOSSLE To entangle, to confuse business

WAIN-COCK A wagon-load of hay
WALLOP To beat
WAFFERED Fatigued; beaten
WARN, WARND To assure, to make certain, warrant
WEKTHY Soft, pliant, flexible
WET Used as a substantive for rain, 'Come in, out of she
wet'
WHEEDLE To coax, to deceive by flattery
WHELM To overthrow
WHIFFLE To move lightly
WHOAM Home
WIMMIN Women
WINDER Window
WILL-GILL An effeminate person
WIT-WALL The large black and white woodpecker
WOMEN-YOLK Women
WONDERMENT, 'OOMDERMENT Anything not
understood
WORDLED The world
WORSEN To make worse

YAFFERN An apron
YEAWS Ewes
YARDS Herbs
YELT A young sow
YEMATH Latter-gross after mowing
YETTIN, YETTING Forming, coming together
YOPPING, YOPPETING Dogs barking

ZENNERS Sinews
ZOG To soak
ZUVRIN Sovereign, a gold £1 coin
ZWATHE (SWATHE) Grass when first mowed

Sources & Photograph Details

TEXT

All of the pages number given below relate to pages in this book, and not the page numbers of the source books.

The main sources for descriptive text are Alfred Williams and J. Arthur Gibbs: Alfred Williams *Round About Middle Thames* pp. 34, 57, 62, 64, 94, 95, 102, 103, 108 and 113, *In a Wiltshire Village* pp. 14, 17, 42, 49, 54, 77, 78, 82, 100 and 116; Joseph Arthur Gibbs *A Cotswold Village* pp. 18, 53, 69, 88 and 105. Other works used are: S.S. Buckman *John Darke's Sojourn on Cotteswolds and Elsewhere* pp. 19 and 76; Laurie Lee *Cider with Rosie* pp. 32 and 73; John Drinkwater *Cotswold Characters* pp. 79 and 92; G. Edmund Hall *Willum Workman's Wit and Wisdom* pp. 59 and 119; Major Gambier Parry *Allegories of the Land* p. 50; *The Spirit of the Old Folk* p. 97; Mary Sturge Gretton *A Corner of the Cotswolds* p. 111 *Burford Past and Present*, p. 111; Paul Hawkins Fisher *Notes and Recollections of Stroud* pp. 13 and 36; William Plomer (ed.) *Kilvert Diaries* p. 48; P. Bonthron *My Holiday on English Waterways* p. 23; E. Temple Thurston *The Flower of Gloster* p. 27; John Henry Garrett *From a Cotswold Height* p. 44; Howard Williams *Diary of a Rowing Tour* p. 55; Edmund Gosse *Father and Son* p. 56; F. Tomson-Smythe *Chronicles of Shortwood* p. 56; B.H. Blacker & W.P.W. Phillimore (eds.) *Gloucestershire Notes & Queries* vols i - vii pp. 61, 89, 90 and 91; John Moore *Portrait of Elmbury*, p. 84; Fred Archer *The Village Doctor* p. 89; David Verey (ed.) *The Diary of a Victorian Squire* pp. 8 snd 91.

Newspapers include *The Tetbury Advertiser* 1886 p. 13, 1888 p. 36; *The Gloucester Journal* pp. 91 and 115; *The Wilts. & Glos. Standard* p. 22; Periodical *Sunday At Home* August 1890 p. 45.

Government Reports include *Report on the Condition of the Handloom Weavers* pp. 4 and 7; *First Report of the Royal Commission on the Employment of Children* p. 22.

Manuscript memoirs include Miss E.M. Bengough *Childhood at the Ridge* p. 37 (courtesy Mr R. Chidlaw); William Smith *Reminiscences from Witney* p. 101 (courtesy Oxfordshire County Library & Museum Service); Thomas Bonting *Reminiscences of Emigration from Filkins* p. 115 (courtesy Oxfordshire County Library & Museum Services).

ILLUSTRATIONS

The credits and information on all of the illustrations used in this book are given in page ascending sequence. Where a source is referred to frequently, only initials are used, and the key to these is at the end of this section. Where dates are known, or reasonably easily deduced by the owners of the pictures, these have been given.

Page 1, half-title, Boating on Pittville Lake, Cheltenham, c. 1905; *Cheltenham Museum & Art Gallery*. Page 2, Children at Holywell Farm Lane, Oakridge, c. 1910; *SG*. Manoeuvres at Westhall Hill Triangle, Fulbrook near Burford, 1909; *Alfred Jewell*. Page 3, title page, High Street, Bourton-on-the-Water, 1895; *OCL*. Page 4, The Ormond's Head, Tetbury, c. 1880; *John Phillips*. Page 5, Employees of William Selwyn's flock mill at Toadsmoor, early 1990s; *SG*. Page 6, Gloucester docks, c. 1880; *Brian Frith*. Page 8, Cloth racks (tenters) of Seville's Mill, Chalford, 1860; *SG*. Page 9, Children at Gloucester docks, 1880; *Brian Frith*. Monk's Mill, Alderley, c. 1870; *Donald Emes*. Page 10, Pencil inscription on timber removed from Hawkwood College, Stroud, dated to 1845; *B.J. Nesfield-Cookson*. Long Street, Dursley, c. 1900; *AS*. Page 12, Union Street, Dursley, with a distant view of the Workhouse matron leading the white corduroy-clad inmates down to Church, c. 1890; *David B. Evans*. Page 13, The Slad, Boulton Lane and Union Street committee for celebrating the coronation of Edward VII, 1902. The 'Grande Dame' is Betsy Cross, the right-hand of the two older ladies at the front. Louisa Sutton, then Hancock, is at the very end on the right-hand side; *AS*. Page 15, Joseph and Louisa Sutton pictured in Boulton Lane, Dursley on their wedding day, Christmas Day 1903; *AS*. Page 17, Mount Street, Gloucester, 1880; *Brian Frith*. Page 18, Advertisements from the *Gloucester Journal* for 1894; *CC*. Page 19, Harper Street (now West Street), Tetbury, c. 1900; *John Phillips*. Page 20, Upper Cam, c. 1900; *David E. Evans*. Page 21, Market House, Minchinhampton; *WM*. Page 22, Pigs in the street, Chipping Campden; *GRO*. High Street, Stroud, c. 1902; *SC*. Page 23, High Street, Burford, 1910; *Alfred Jewell*. Page 24, High Street, Northleach, c. 1900; *OCL*. Page 25, Threshing in a barn at Great Barrington, c. 1895; *OCL*. Page 26, High Street, Moreton-in-Marsh, taken from the corner of Oxford Street, c. 1890; *OCL*. Page 27, High Street, Northleach, 1901; *OCL*. Page 28, The New Inn, Bisley, (now the Stirrup Cup), c. 1905; *SC*. Page 30, St John's Lock, Lechlade c. 1870; *OCL*. The Trout Inn, Lechlade; *PG*. Page 31, The canal bridge and the Bricklayers Arms, viewed from the bottom of Daneway Hilt, c. 1905; *SC*. The west portal of Sapperton Tunnel, 1911,

with a party of local trippers; *SC*. Page 32, The Thames near Kempsford, c. 1883; *OCL*. The Thames and Severn Canal at Cerney Lock, c. 1883; *OCL*. Page 33, Wharf Lock and Wharf Cottage at Daneway, c. 1904; *OCL*. The *Balgonie* on the Thames and Severn Canal in the Golden Valley, c. 1910; *AS*. Page 34, The Thames and Severn Canal at Chalford; *SC*. Chalford, the continuation of the High Street to the east of Coppice Hill, down Tanner's Pitch to the entrance to Dimmesdale and Ashmeads; *SC*. Page 35, Coal delivery by donkey, Coppice Hill, Chalford, c. 1905; *SC*. Page 36, Cowswell Spring, Bussage; *SC*. Page 37, Wharf Cottage and Daneway Basin, c. 1904; *SC*. Page 38, The Bricklayers Arms, Daneway, 8 May 1917; *SC*. Sapperton Tunnel, some time before canal closure in 1911; *SC*. Page 39, The Holy Well, Oakridge; *SC*. Page 40, A scene near Oakridge; *WM*. Page 41, Mary Twissel's Cottage in Twissels Hill, Oakridge, c. 1900; *SC*. Page 42, Cottage at Laverton, c. 1860; *David Aldred*. Page 44, Station Road, Stow-on-the-Wold; *CCC*. Page 45, East side of The Ridge, with orangery, c. 1905; *Donald Emes*. The Bengough twins, c. 1872; *Richard Chidlaw*. Page 46, Painswick, August 1890; *CRO*. Page 47, The gardeners at Sherborne; *CCC & Mrs W.C. George*. Page 48, Members of the Mitford family riding on the estate at Batsford Park; *CCC & Hon. Mrs Pamela Jackson*. Page 49, The 2nd Volunteer Battalion of the Gloucestershire Regiment at camp, c. 1885; *AS*. Page 50, View of Lechlade from Highworth Road, c. 1885; *OCL*. Page 51, The Puesdown Inn; *PC*. The Toadsmoor Valley; *SC*. Page 53, Driveway to Dovedale House, Blockley, c. 1895; *OCL*. Page 54, Dursley Union Workhouse; *David E. Evans*. Page 55, Castle Street, Cirencester, 1901; *OCL*. Page 56, One-up, one-down cottages, with residents, thought to be at Clapham, Gloucester; *Jill Voyce*. Page 57, Bringing in the hay at Batsford; *CCC*. Page 58, Vicarage Street, Painswick, c. 1905; *GRO*. Page 59, Lady Juliana's Gateway, Chipping Campden House, c. 1895; *OCL*. Page 60, John and Mary Hall attending a point-to-point as Bledington Grounds, c. 1922; *CCC & Bledington Local History Society*. Page 61, Farm scene at Batsford; *CCC*. London Street, c. 1900; *Edwin Cuss*. Page 62, The Chedworth Band, 1905; *CCC & The late Mrs Day, Chedworth*. Court Farm, Chipping Campden; *CCC*. Page 65, Tewkesbury, c. 1880; *AC. Hilton*. Page 66, A baptism at Cricklade, c. 1895; *PG*. Page 67, Bibury, c. 1895; *OCL*. Page 68, A group at Miserden; *WM*. A scene outside a beerhouse at Compton Abdale; *PG*. Page 69, Charles Andrews of Willersey, market gardener, selling asparagus door-to-door, c. 1900; *CCC & Museum of English Rural Life*. Page 70, The Fleece Inn, Chalford, with coal-delivery donkeys standing at the end of Commercial Road; *SC*. Page 71, Wragg Castle Farm, Pitchcombe, c. 1880; *CC*. Page 72, Fairford; *Edwin Cuss*. Page 73, Arlington Row, Bibury,

1901; *OCL*. Page 75, Arlington Mill, Bibury; *CCC*. Page 76, Bibury from Arlington Bridge, August 1906; *OCL*. Bibury looking towards Arlington Bridge and the Swan Hotel, 1901; *OCL*. Page 77, Team of four oxen on the Cotswolds from Packer's Country Life series; *CCC*. Page 78, Cottage at Lilfield near Stroud, 1905; from *Old Cottages, Farm-houses and other Stone Buildings in the Cotswold District*, W. Galsworthy Davie. Page 79, Carter's Boys, Packer's Country Life series; *CCC*. Page 80, Relaxation after work. A carter, horses and boy, from Packer's Country Life series; *CCC*. Page 81, A carter with horse teams and boys; *CCC*. Page 83, A horse bus outside the Lenthall Temperance Hotel, Sheep Street, Burford in the 1890s; *Alfred Jewell*. Page 84, Burford Hiring Fair, outside the Lamb Hotel, Sheep Street, Burford, *c.* 1910; *CCC*. Page 85, Agricultural labourers with three separate horse teams; *CCC*. Page 86, The ford, Shipton Oliffe, 1905; *OCL*. Page 87, Mickleton, with the church of St Lawrence in the background, *c.* 1898; *OCL*. A Cottage at Chedworth; from *Old Cottages, Farm-houses and other Stone Buildings in the Cotswold District*, W. Galsworthy Davie. Page 88, The Club Day celebrations at Ebrington; *CCC*. Page 89, Gleaners at Blockley; *CCC*. Mrs Watkins and grand-daughter Emmie gleaning at Forthampton near Tewkesbury, 1905; *A.C. Hilton*. Page 90, Kingscourt, Stroud; *WM*. Page 91, The Old Coffee Tavern, Chalford, *c.* 1905; *SG*. Page 92, Smithy at Coln St Aldwyn; *CCC*. Page 93, The Black Horse, North Nibley, *c.* 1915; *AS*. A country lane, entitled by the photographer 'The Wood Manor House'; *WM*. Page 95, Blackley, *c.* 1895; *OCL*. Thomas Moss, a labourer at Brookthorpe, *c.* 1880; *GC*. Page 96, Burford Street, Lechlade, *c.* 1905; *OCL*. Page 97, 'Bangem' Barrett, a vegetable seller from Marston Meysey, selling vegetables in Fairford, 1911; *Edwin Cuss*. Page 98, Apple harvesters at Aldertan *c.* 1912; *David Aldred*. A Great Western Railway carrier at Cirenrester; *PG*. Page 99, Working in a weaving shed, 1898; *Tom Worley*. Blankets being hung on tenterhooks to stretch and dry, 1898; *Tom Worley*. Page 100, New Street and the Falcon Hotel, Painswick, *c.* 1904; *Donald Emes*. A street cleaning party, Painswick, *c.* 1900; *CRO*. Page 101, Thames Head, fourth spring and pump at Coates. Note pumping station for canal in background; *OCL*. Page 102, The River Coln at Fairford, *c.* 1890; *OCL*. Page 103, Harvesting near King's Stanley; *WM*. Page 104, Market Square, Stow-on-the-Wold, *c.* 1885; *OCL*. Page 106, Kemble Bridge, *c.* 1883; *OCL*. Page 107, The ruins of the Pest House in Waterlane, Oakridge, following the disturbances of 1895 against the intended movement there of the Stroud smallpox victims; *SC*. Page 108, Haymaking scene, *c.* 1880; *CCC*. Page 109, Park Farm, Blockley, 1906; *CCC*. Page 110, Farming scene at Fairford; *CCC*. Page 111, Anzac soldiers helping out on a farm near Tetbury, *c.* 1915; *Jean Price*. The miller calls; *CCC*. Page 112, A mower sharpening his scythe; *CCC*. Page 113, Shredding mangolds for cattle feed, *c.* 1905; *Museum of English Rural Life, Reading*. Page 115, Scene at Frogmarsh, Woodchester; *WM*. Outside the general stores, Oakridge; *SG*. Page 116, Celebrating the relief of Mafeking in Burford, 1900; *Museum of English Rural Life, Reading*. Page 117, Cottages at Ebrington; from *Old Cottages, Farm-houses and other Stone Buildings in the Cotswold District*, W. Galsworthy Davie. Page 118, Steam power on a farm at Hailey; *CCC*. Page 119, Lower Well, Stow-on-the-Wold, *c.* 1888; *OCL*. Page 120, Chedworth Roman Villa; *PG*. Page 122, The River Coln at Fairford, *c.* 1888; *OCL*. Page 123, The River Coln at Fairford, *c.* 1888; *OCL*. A scene at Fairford; *Edwin Cuss*. Page 124, The head of the Coln at Andoversford, *c.* 1885; *OCL*. Page 125, The King's Head Inn, Bledington Green; *CCC*. Cricklade Street, Cirencester, 1903; *OCL*. Page 126, Nailsworth, looking towards Watledge; *CRO*. Ludgate Hill, Wotton-under-Edge, *c.* 1900; *Donald Emes*. Page 127 Burford Post Office; *Alfred Jewell*. Page 128, Tenants outside the cottages in College Yard, Burford; *Alfred Jewell*. Page 129, Chippenham Platt coal wharf, Eastington; *SC*. Page 130, Street scene at South Cerney; *PC*. Page 131, Haywain on the Malmesbury Road, Cricklade; *PG*. Page 132, Farm workers in a barn at Great Barrington, *c.* 1895; *OCL*. Page 133, A view across a wheatfield at Lower Slaughter, *c.* 1890; *OCL*. A sand delivery man camping out, *c.* 1880; *GC*. Page 134, Great Rissingson, *c.* 1893; *OCL*. Gypsy Pegler of Painswick; *SG*. Page 135, Bridge over the Windrush. at Lower Guiting, *c.* 1895; *OCL*. The River Eye at Lower Slaughter; *CCC*. Page 136, The Severn Vale from Rodborough; *WM*. Page 137, The Bear Inn, Stroud Road, Bisley; *SG*. Spring at Far Oakridge; *SG*. Page 138, Church Steps, Bisley; *WM*. Cottages at Tunley, *c.* 1890; *SG*.

Key: AS Alan Sutton, author collection. *CCC* Cotswold Countryside Collection, Cotswold District Council, Northleach. *GC* Gloucestershire Collection, Gloucestershire County Library, City Library, Brunswick Road, Gloucester. *OCL* Oxfordshire County Library and Museum Services, City Library, Westgate, Oxford. *PG* Philip Griffiths. *SC* Stanley Gardiner. *WM* Wilfred Merrett.